# Southern African National Liberation Movements and the Campaign for Representation in the United Nations, 1962-1975

Adonis & Abbey Publishers Ltd
Third Floor
207 Regent Street
London W1B 3HH
Website: http://www.adonis-abbey.com
E-mail Address: editor@adonis-abbey.com

Nigeria:
Unit 1, Vintage Hill Estate Plot No 1368, Guzape District,
Abuja, Nigeria
Tel: +234 7058078841, 234 8052213212
Copyright 2025 © Seane Mabitsela

British Library Cataloguing-in-Publication Data
A catalogue record for this book is available from the British Library

ISBN: 9781913976729

The moral right of the author has been asserted

All rights reserved. No part of this book may be reproduced, stored in a retrieval system or transmitted at any time or by any means without the prior permission of the publisher

# Southern African National Liberation Movements and the Campaign for Representation in the United Nations, 1962-1975

Seane Mabitsela (PhD)

# Table of Contents

Acknowledgements .................................................................................... ix

Foreword .................................................................................................... xi

List of Acronyms/Definitions/Abbreviations ....................................... xiii

## CHAPTER ONE

1.1. Introduction ........................................................................................ 15

1.2. Study Overview .................................................................................. 17

## CHAPTER TWO

### The UN Practice for Representation of National Liberation Movements, 1962-1974 ............................................................................ 23

2.1. Introduction ........................................................................................ 23

Diagram 1: UN practice for representation of National Liberation Movements (NLMs) ................................................................................. 24

2.2. UN Consideration of the Territories in Africa, 1962-1974 ............ 26

2.2.1. Fourth Committee of the GA ........................................................ 26

2.2.2. Special Committee on the Granting of Independence to Colonial Countries and Peoples ............................................................................ 34

2.2.3. UN Council for Namibia ................................................................ 40

2.2.4. UN Economic Commission for Africa .......................................... 43

2.3. Conclusion .......................................................................................... 47

## CHAPTER 3

### UN Reactions and Responses to the Representation of National Liberation Movements ...... 49

3.1. Introduction ...... 49

3.2. The GA decisions on acknowledging the role of liberation movements in decolonisation ...... 51

3.3 Conclusion ...... 76

## CHAPTER FOUR

### The Role of OAU on Representation of National Liberation Movements at the UN, 1963-1974 ...... 79

4.1. Introduction ...... 79

4.2. The OAU Executive Council Decisions on the Support and Assistance for the National Liberation Movements, 1963-1974 ...... 81

4.3. Conclusion ...... 104

## CHAPTER FIVE

### The Effects of Representation of National Liberation Movements at the UN ...... 105

5.1. Introduction ...... 105

Diagram 2: Stages for the representation of national liberation movements in the UN ...... 107

5.2. Effects of the Representation of National Liberation Movements at the UN ...... 108

5.2.1. The First Session of the Diplomatic Conference on the Reaffirmation and Development of IHL Applicable in Armed Conflicts ...... 108

5.2.2. United Nations Conference on the Representation of States' Relations with International Organisations ..................................................................115

5.2.3. The World Conference on International Women's Year ................122

5.3 Conclusion ..................................................................................125

**CHAPTER SIX**

**Summary, Evaluation and Conclusion** ..................................127

6.1. Summary ..................................................................................127

6.2. Evaluation ................................................................................128

6.3. Conclusion ...............................................................................130

**References** ..................................................................................137

**Index** ..........................................................................................151

# Acknowledgements

I extend immense gratitude to Professors Patrick Dzimiri and Tendai Chari for their expert guidance and support in this venture. Their comprehensive review, from beginning to end, provided comments that significantly shape this study. To their persistence, they added the most generous offer of help.

It was an exhilarating experience, working in association with the following people during the preparation of this study: Ephraim Yende (University of Mpumalanga); Lesiba Mashishi (University of Venda); and Mahunele Thotse (University of Limpopo). Their amazing encouragement is acknowledged. I especially enjoyed their company, discussions, and their comments during the study. I would like to thank them for their incessant conversations and commitment to their work in various fields.

Finally, I would like to thank my editor, Dr Mouzayian Khali (University of Warwick, United Kingdom) and the publishers (Adonis and Abbey, United Kingdon & Nigeria) for attending to the copy-editing, proofreading, and formatting the study.

# Foreword

This study comprises six chapters of varying length. The chapters are organised chronologically and thematically. This indicates the narrative may, at times, adopt a historical thematic approach. This study's periodisation, which dictates chapter separation, is based on identifying six distinct chapters. Chapter One provides an introduction and background, methodology for the entire study. Chapter Two covers the practice for representation of national liberation movements at the UN. The chapter's first section is an introduction. It then moves to explore, in the second place, the UN consideration of the territories in Africa, to describe that practice. It delves into the deliberations and proceedings of the General Assembly's (GA) main organs—the Fourth Committee, Special Committee on Independence, UN Council for Namibia, and the Economic Commission of Africa (ECA) to reveal the practice. The last section summarises and provides highlights emanating from the main discussion. Chapter Three addresses UN reactions and responses to the representation of national liberation movements during the period between 1962 and 1974. It first introduces the subject, then explores GA decisions to describes reactions and responses. The concluding section of the chapter summarises and provides the main highlights from the discussion. Chapter Four examines the role of the OAU in the representation of national liberation movements at the UN during the period between 1963 and 1974. It starts with a brief introduction and proceeds to explore decisions of the Organisation of African Unity (OAU) Executive Council—Assembly of Heads of States and Government and the Council of Ministers, to describe the role. The last section of the chapter presents the summary of the discussion. Chapter Five examines the effects of the representation of African national liberation movements in the UN. First, it introduces the subject and then proceeds explore some case examples of the UN-organised conferences, to describe those effects. Main highlights and a summary of the discussion are presented in the last section of the chapter. The Sixth and final chapter presents a summative evaluation and conclusion.

# List of Acronyms/Definitions/Abbreviations

| | |
|---|---|
| ANC | African National Congress |
| ANCZ | African National Congress Zimbabwe |
| COREMO | Revolutionary Committee of Mozambique |
| DRC | Democratic Republic of the Congo |
| ECA | Economic Commission for Africa |
| ECOSOC | Economic and Social Council |
| FAO | Food and Agricultural Organisation |
| FNLA | National Front for the Liberation of Angola |
| FOFATUSA | Federation of Free Trade Unions of South Africa |
| FRELIMO | National Front for the Liberation of Mozambique |
| GA | General Assembly |
| GRAE | Revolutionary Government of Angola in Exile |
| IACW | International American Commission on Women |
| IADB | Inter-America Development Bank |
| IBRD | International Bank for Reconstruction and Development |
| ICJ | International Court of Justice |
| ICRC | International Committee of the Red Cross |
| IHL | International Humanitarian Law |
| IDAF | International Defence Aid Fund |
| ILC | International Law Commission |
| ILO | International Labour Organisation |
| IMCO | Inter-governmental Consultative Organisation |
| IMF | International Monetary Fund |
| MLGP | Movement for the Liberation of Portuguese Guinea |
| MONLIGO | National Liberation Movement for the Liberation of the Comoro |
| MPLA | Popular Movement for the Liberation of Angola |
| NATO | North Atlantic Treaty Organisation |
| NLMs | National Liberation Movements |
| OAU | Organisation of African Unity |
| OLA | Office of Legal Affairs |
| OPEC | Organisation of Petroleum Exporting Countries |
| PAC | Pan Africanist Congress |
| PAIGC | African Party for the Independence of Guinea and Cape Verde |

| | |
|---|---|
| PLO | Palestinian Liberation Organisation |
| PRC | People's Republic of China |
| RSA | Republic of South Africa |
| SC | Security Council |
| SUP | Seychelles United Party |
| SWANU | South West African National Union |
| SWAPO | South West Africa People's Organisation |
| TRC | Truth and Reconciliation |
| UK | United Kingdom |
| UN | United Nations |
| UNDP | United Nations Development Programme |
| UNESCO | United Nations Educational, Scientific and Cultural Organisation |
| UNHCR | United Nations High Commissioner for Refugees |
| UNICEF | United Nations Children's Emergency Fund |
| USSR | Union of Soviet Socialist Republic |
| WHO | World Health Organisation |
| ZANU | Zimbabwean African National Union |
| ZAPU | Zimbabwean African People's Union |

# CHAPTER ONE

## 1.1 Introduction

The representation of revolutionary or liberation movements in international organisations of a universal character such as the United Nations (UN), strengthens cooperation. Southern African national liberation movements' representation at the UN from 1962 to 1975 is an issue that calls for a scholarly analysis. Studying the history of liberation movements' UN representation requires understanding decolonisation, especially the 1960 Declaration of Independence or Decolonisation. The Declaration was an important stage in the development of international law governing the non-self-governing or non-independent territories; and, served as the legal basis for the process of decolonisation (Shaw, 1983). Its significance and subsequent history operated as its title suggested, within the framework of granting independence to colonial countries or peoples (Ibid).

Contextually, Southern African national liberation movements refer to the dominant and competitive movements from non-self-governing or non-dependent territories in Africa, as defined in the UN Charter (UN Charter, 1945). The non-self-governing territories included Angola, Namibia, Zimbabwe, Mozambique, among others, in Africa. Together, the liberation movements were recognised by the Organisation of African Unity (OAU) as the authentic representatives of the peoples in colonial territories (Temu, 2014).

Recognition by OAU of the liberation movements was one of the Organisation's diplomatic weapons for their support and assistance at the global level (Boavida, et.al. 2010). However, the OAU's major diplomatic actions would be carried out by the African Group at the UN. Comprised of the permanent representatives of all the 54 African Union member states, the Group was created in 1963 at the behest of the OAU to promote African interests at the UN (Paterson & Virk, 2013).

In 1962, when the UN started to consider territories in Africa for speeding up the decolonisation process, members of the national liberation movements were working as 'petitioners' or 'private individuals' (Shaw, 183) within its system. In 1972, the UN General Assembly (GA) authorised its committees to associate the liberation movements recognised by OAU with the Assembly's work. The association of the movements with the work of the Assembly was conducted in consultation with OAU because the latter pressured it [Assembly] to recognise movements fighting against colonial domination, alien occupation and racist regimes on behalf of their people's right to self-determination (Esterhuyse, 1989). By this decision, the ANC and PAC, two relevant movements from South Africa were invited to participate in the GA Special Political Committee's debates on the policies of apartheid of the Government of South Africa in the capacity of observer (GA SPC, 1974). The Special Political Committee also recommended that the GA make the necessary financial provision to enable the representatives of those movements to do so (Ibid).

Although the GA had endorsed the decision of its main committees relating to the representation of the national liberation movements in their proceedings, attempts to persuade a declaration before it by Amilcar Cabral, leader of the African Party for the Independence of Guinea-Bissau and Cape Verde (PAIGC) movement in Guinea-Bissau failed (Shaw, 1983). It must be stressed that Guinea-Bissau (West Africa) is not in Southern Africa. It is mentioned here because the national liberation movements from there had a connection with those in Angola and Mozambique, and that it was a Portuguese administered territory.

Cabral's declaration had been communicated to the Assembly on 8 January 1973 before his death on 20 January (Houser & Henderson, 1973) the same year. Further tries in that regard were rendered futile by the April 1974 coup in Portugal. This coup threatened the viability of the citadels of white power in Southern Africa and signalled the eminence of full independence for Mozambique and Angola (Strategic Survey, 1974).

However, in a dramatic move, the GA invited Palestinian Liberation Organisation (PLO) leader, Yasser Arafat to deliver a speech in November 1974. An extract of his speech read: "great numbers of peoples, including those of Zimbabwe, Namibia, South Africa and Palestine, among many others, were still victims of oppression and violence; and that the international community needed to support those peoples in their struggles, in the furtherance of their rightful causes and the attainment of their right to self-determination" (Arafat, 1974). Arafat's speech was interrupted nine times by applause. However, when he finished a large audience of the GA gave him a standing ovation that lasted for two minutes (Hoffman, 1974). Based on Arafat's speech, the Assembly, in an analogous but more far-reaching move adopted a resolution 3236 (XXIX) inviting the PLO to participate in its sessions and, in the same capacity, in international conferences organised under the auspices of the UN (UN YB, 1974).

The difference between the PLO and African liberation movements related to representation in areas not related to their respective countries. The PLO's representation was a mark of the political influence that could be mobilized on behalf of the organisation, particularly within the UN (Shaw, 1983).

Although differences existed between the representation of African liberation movements and the PLO in committees and organs of the UN, a precedent and a major change appeared to have been established concerning the status of the liberation movements in global affairs.

## 1.2 Study Overview

National liberation movements are a colossal theme in African history. Yet, despite the huge amount of written work on the subject, there is a surprisingly lack of extensive and detailed research on regional national liberation movements as a single entity in the UN. This thesis examines the representation of Southern African national liberation movements at the UN from 1962 to 1975. It explores the UN's practice regarding national liberation movement representation, the UN's evolving reactions and responses to it, the OAU's role in facilitating this representation, and the overall effects of on the movements' representation at the UN, as well as the effects for the representation of the movements at the UN. These are some of the aspects that have not been scholarly scrutinised and analysed in existing literature on the subject. Scrutinising and analysing them is important because it exposes the national liberation movements' role in helping and supporting the international political plane to speed up the process of decolonisation in general.

The study contributes broadly to understanding the battles fought by Southern African national liberation movements at the diplomatic level and their role in decolonisation. Hence, it makes a significant contribution to African history, stimulating further research interest in the subject and future publications. It is also hoped that this study will be of value to scholars interested not only in the history of the national liberation movements generally but with the evolution of the UN as a guardian of the people's legitimate rights to independence, self-determination and freedom; and that the future volumes and monographs will sustain the momentum and contribute to a growing field of inquiry that can only increase in importance: the dialectics of globalisation. However, it must, be noted that the discourses of the rights to independence, self-determination and freedom in the UN were replete with vested interest under the disguise of moral concerns and were occasioned mainly by the prevalence of ideological struggles better known as the "Cold War" between the West led by the United States (US) and the East led by the then Soviet Union and allies (Ade-Ibijola & Mngomezulu, 2020). For the anti-colonial powers in general, those discourses were a success for the framers of the UN. Their major impact was establishing decolonisation as a top priority in international affairs, providing the GA with tools to end colonialism, and ensuring the struggle for self-determination and formal political independence could no longer be ignored (Gouraige, 1974).

Southern African national liberation movements are the focus of this study. In particular, the study focuses, among others, on the Front for the Liberation of Mozambique (FRELIMO); South West Africa People's Organisation (SWAPO); Zimbabwean African People's Union (ZAPU) and Zimbabwe African National Union (ZANU); African National Congress (ANC) and Pan Africanist Congress (PAC) of South Africa; Popular Movement for the Liberation of Angola (MPLA) and the National Front for the Liberation of Angola (FNLA).

The period covered by this study is 1962 to 1975. As stated earlier, the year 1962 is significant because it coincided with the UN Special Committee of 24' start of the implementation of the 1960 Declaration on the Granting of Independence to Colonial Countries and Peoples [Declaration on Decolonisation] (UN YB, 1960). Specifically, in February 1962, the UN Special Committee decided to hear petitioners from colonial territories, including those in Africa. Most petitioners originated from the national liberation movements of those territories. Once again, as indicated, the year 1975 is significant because it marked the start of independence for Angola and Mozambique, followed by Zimbabwe in 1980, Namibia in 1990, and South Africa in 1994 (Mbandlwa, 2023).

It is also vital to state why research the subject of national liberation movements. Research on national liberation movements abounds, but most writers and scholars have focused their attention on individual national liberation movements' relationship with the UN. Despite these proliferations, historical research, and incisive analysis of liberation movements of the region, particularly their activities as a single entity at the international level during the clandestine period of their existence, are sparse and insufficient. While several historians and political scientists have researched liberation movements, few of them have focused their attention on the liberation movements of the Southern African region as a single entity's involvement with the UN.

By contrast, the present study shows how the seed of representation of the national liberation movements of the Southern African region germinated in international institutions, particularly at the UN. It explores the diplomatic strategies Southern African national liberation movements, as a single entity, used to mobilise aid and support for their struggles. The way the movements' battles were fought at the diplomatic level and the international community's feelings towards them, especially the administering powers are some of the aspects that have not been scrutinised and analysed. Scrutinising and analysing these aspects are important because it exposes the national liberation movements' role in helping and supporting the international political plane to speed up the process of decolonisation in general.

Although literature on the national liberation movements abounds, little has been written on the representation of Southern African national liberation movements as a single entity at the UN. This gap reflects 'different perspectives' and 'shifting interests' on the part of recent scholars on the issue. The different perspectives on the subject have been facilitated partly by the establishment of new specialist journals and the availability of records on the subject in the preceding years (Saunders, 2009); while the shifting interests have been facilitated partly by historical topics emanating from the secondary sources suiting the writers' views, especially their conversance with prominent historiographical debates of their own time Cowgill & Waring (2017).

Given the above, this study enters the discussion within the framework of different perspectives and shifting interests on the subject to analyse the representation of Southern African national liberation at the UN from 1962 to 1975. It answers: How did the international community respond to national liberation movement representation at the UN? What was the OAU's role in this representation? What were the effects of this representation? Answering these pertinent questions is important because they reveal the significant role of the national liberation movements of the region as a single entity on the international political plane as far as the process of decolonisation was concerned, especially the eventual independence and freedom of the people in their respective territories led by the movements.

This study used qualitative methods to research and analyse the representation of southern African national liberation movements at the UN from 1962 to 1975. Qualitative research method is important because it provides specific and deep information processing about relationships with performance and offers a holistic understanding of human experience within a particular setting (Rahman, 2017). In this instance, the qualitative research approach enabled the author to analyse the social, economic, and political hurdles that confronted the Southern African national liberation movements at the diplomatic level during the period under review. The author also consulted the *UN Digital Library* and *World Legal Institute* to locate decisions of the world body on decolonisation, especially on apartheid and colonialism at the height of national liberation struggles in Southern Africa.

Most primary sources came from the UN General Assembly (New York) and OAU Secretariat (Addis Ababa) documents. Primary sources which were consulted include declarations, resolutions, recommendations, annexes, and agenda items. All these provided useful information on how the UN and the OAU dealt with events concerning the liberation movements as they unfolded during the period under review. The major weakness of sources of this kind of study is that they are official and therefore reflect the views of the office-bearers concerning the politics of the day. This gap was partially bridged by using publications such as *Sechaba*. First published in January 1967, *Sechaba* was the Official organ of the ANC of South Africa but also captured the voices of liberation movements in Namibia, Angola, Mozambique and Zimbabwe and their official stance on world affairs.

Other sources essential to the study were the national liberation movements' memoranda and statements before the UN. The value of all these is that they highlighted collective actions of the national liberation movements of the region on a world stage, alongside member states of the world body. But at the same time, these memoranda and statements also reflected liberation movements' individual views rather than the actual external realities of their struggles. This study also received help from a host of internet sources. These sources are rich in activities of the national liberation movements at the international level, especially during the period under review.

Apart from the above sources, the study also used published works such as reports, books, and journals. The *Yearbook of the United Nations* proved to be especially useful because it has sessions of the world organisation of which the national liberation movements were part. This was an extremely valuable source for the study. The *Yearbook of the United Nations* yields vital information concerning debates on decolonisation and decisions regarding colonialism and apartheid. Its strength lies in expressing the international community's view on decolonisation, including support for liberation movements' struggles against colonialism and apartheid in Southern Africa during the review period. This includes the support and aid for the liberation movements' struggles against colonialism and apartheid in the Southern African region during the period under review.

The study further benefited from Official Records of the UN GA, Security Council (SC), and the Economic and Social Council (ECOSOC), as well as Conferences organised under the world body's auspices. In general, the UN Official Records consist of meeting records (of the main bodies) and supplements, including reports of subsidiary bodies and resolutions and decisions of the Assembly, and other selected documents, such as agenda items and annexes. Official records were used in the study due to their comprehensive coverage of African affairs, including detailed accounts of national liberation movements in UN proceedings and deliberations on colonial affairs. Some of the information in these records could not be accessed in other ways. But the major strength of the UN Official Records is that they capture events that involved the liberation movements, as they occur within the world body.

# CHAPTER TWO

## The UN Practice for Representation of National Liberation Movements, 1962-1974

### 2.1 Introduction

This chapter concerns the practice of representation of national liberation movements in the UN. It is divided into three sections. The first section introduces the subject of practice for representation of national liberation movements at the UN. Section two explores consideration by UN committees or organs: the Fourth Committee of the GA; the Special Committee on the Granting of Independence to Colonial Countries and Peoples; the UN Council for Namibia; and the UN Economic Commission for Africa (ECA) of the question of Zimbabwe, Mozambique, Angola and Namibia, to describe that practice. The third section concludes the chapter.

In the years between 1945 and 1972, there were no explicit provisions or pertinent rules of procedure for the representation of national liberation movements at the UN. The representation of liberation movements was based on established practice, following the authorised decisions by the GA and ECOSOC. *Inter alia*, the following practice seemed to have been applied: the representatives of liberation movements were invited through the OAU, and invitations were transmitted by the Secretary-General after the decision to invite them had been taken by the relevant GA organ or committee; the representatives of the movements were seated in the rooms in seats designed as 'observers' and addressed or spoke when permitted to speak during the course of debates relating to their territories; and that they were accorded distribution of certain documents similar to those of the members of the committees' organs; communications from a liberation movement were circulated under cover note from the Chairmen of the committees or organs stating their request; and financial provision for the movements' representation and participation was authorised by the Assembly (UN JYB, 1974). This practice arose primarily from the UN GA organs or committees. Four of these committees or organs were: the Fourth Committee of the GA; the Special Committee on the Granting of Independence to Colonial Countries and Peoples (herein only referred to as Special Committee on Independence/Decolonisation); the UN Council for Namibia; and the UN Economic Commission for Africa (ECA).

**Diagram 1**: UN practice for representation of National Liberation Movements (NLMs)

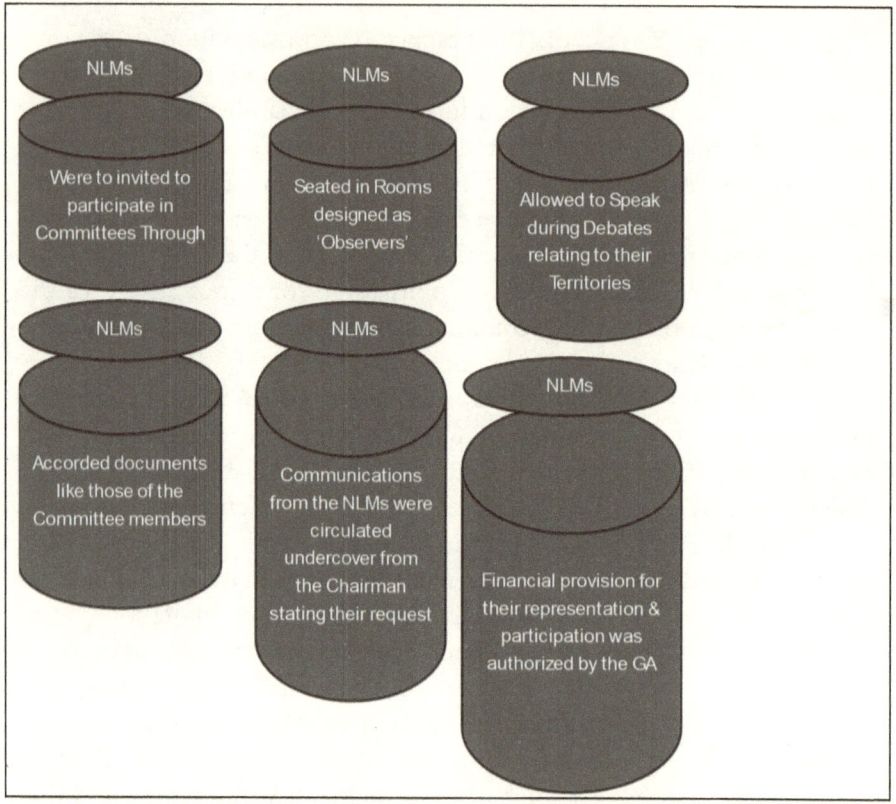

Arguably, the practice set up by these committees or organs allowing representatives of national liberation movements of colonial territories in Africa to take part in their proceedings concerning those territories could be seen as a legitimate move to secure greater information about developments about those territories. Or it could also be seen as an implicit acknowledgement of a kind of superior status with respect for organisations over others and over individuals in such territories where the sources of such information were being unduly restricted (Shaw, 1983).

It appears that the GA and ECOSOC expressly requested UN organs or committees, in consultation with the OAU, to ensure representation of the colonial territories in Africa by national liberation movements, in a suitable capacity, when dealing with matters about those territories. A suitable starting point for understanding the practice for representation of national liberation movements at the UN is to examine the UN GA committees or organs' consideration of the question of African territories in Zimbabwe, Angola, Mozambique, and Namibia. This requires examining the 1962 to 1974 considerations of those committees or organs of those territories.

An analysis of the Assembly committees or organs' consideration of the territories in Africa is critical because they distinguished at the outset which of the national liberation movements were permitted or invited to make statements before the UN organs or committees as 'petitioners' or as individuals or organisations considered capable of furnishing necessary information, or who have appeared before the Security Council (SC) under its rules of procedure as persons considered competent to supply information or give other assistance (UN JYB, 1974).

It is also critical because those organs or committees have presided over the decolonisation of Africa (Scanlon & Murithi, 2009)—thereby further revealing the stages in which the national liberation movements developed a diplomatic struggle against colonial dominance in their respective territories (Santos, 2012). In addition, an analysis of these organs or committees is critical because they provide sources *formelles*—evidence of a recognised source of law in the form of state practice showing the existence of a custom; also contribute to the sources *materielles* of international law; and contribute to the clarification and development of law (Higgins, 1970). Further, their analysis is critical because they became 'focal points of UN anti-colonial activity (Barber, 1975); and reflected and perhaps amplified the ongoing changes of a revolutionary world seeking to be more equitable and democratic at the same time (Fomerand, 1996).

## 2.2 UN Consideration of the Territories in Africa, 1962-1974

### 2.2.1 Fourth Committee of the GA

The GA's Fourth Committee, also known as the Special Political and Decolonisation Committee or SPECPOL or C4 is one of six main committees of the Assembly. Established in 1945, the Committee dealt with a diverse set of political issues, specifically the issue of decolonisation (GA Handbook, 2017). After independence had been granted to all the UN trust territories and the subsequent dismantling of the trusteeship system (NHB, 1951), the Committee's workload decreased.

Consequently, it was merged with the Special Political Committee, which had been created as a seventh main committee to deal with certain political issues (A/RES— 47/233, 1993). The Committee met every year from late September to mid-November but also convened briefly in the Spring to adopt any resolutions and decisions relating to peacekeeping passed by the Special Committee on Peacekeeping Operations. All 193 member states of the UN could attend its meetings (GA Handbook, 2017). Unlike most other UN bodies, the Committee also allowed for petitioners (civil society representatives and other stakeholders) to address decolonisation issues, and adopted resolutions and several draft decisions, usually by consensus (Ibid).

At its twenty-seventh session in 1972, the Fourth Committee of the UN General Assembly addressed the question of African territories, including Zimbabwe, Angola, Mozambique, and South West Africa/Namibia (now Namibia). It had before it a letter from the Chairperson of the Special Committee on Decolonisation/Independence, suggesting that the Fourth Committee consider inviting in consultation with the OAU, representatives of the liberation movements concerned to participate in an observer capacity in the examination of those territories (GA OR, 1972). Since its inception in 1963, OAU regarded the decolonisation of the territories still under colonial domination as the *raison de'tre* and major goal. In particular, the Founding Fathers had deemed it 'imperious and urgent' to support the struggle of those territories (Tekkle, 1988).

The Special Committee approved the Special Committee on Independence's suggestion on 27 September 1972. Following this decision, the following representatives of national liberation movements participated in an observer capacity during the Fourth Committee's discussion of the territories under Portuguese administration: Marcelino dos Santos Vice President, Front for the Liberation of Mozambique (FRELIMO); Mariano Matsinha, member of the Central Committee, FRELIMO; Sharfuddine M. Khan, New York representative; Amilcar Cabral, Secretary-General of the Party for the Independence of Guinea and Cape Verde (PAIGC); Gil Fernandes, member of the Superior Council, PAIGC; and Oscar Teixeira, member of the Executive Committee, PAIGC (GA OR, 1972). The Fourth Committee also heard statements of the following petitioners: Arthur X. L. Vilankulu, Faustino Arvanjo Kambeu and Gwendoline Gumane, Revolutionary Committee of Mozambique (COREMO); and Romesh Chandra, Emilson S. Randriamihasinoro, Gordon Schaefer and Canon Raymond Goor, World Peace Council (ORGA, 1972).

Presumably, the Special Committee's decision to invite the representative was a goodwill gesture by the UN and a show of confidence in those representatives concerning self-determination and independence for colonial countries and people. The decision to allow representatives of the national liberation movements in the Portuguese-administered territories to participate in the discussion as observers was welcomed by many of the Fourth Committee members. For example, Tanzania called the decision to grant them observer status a triumph of common sense and a victory over colonialism (UN YB, 1972).

For the OAU, the decision was historic because it was a result of the long and difficult struggle against colonialism within the framework of the UN, which also led to the recognition of the right of colonial peoples to self-determination and independence and world body recognition of the legitimacy of the struggle of liberation (ORGA, 1972). In addition, the grant of observer status at the UN to liberation movements, considering the recognition by the OAU, 'was certainly a political victory in the drive to internationalise wars of national liberation (Trevona, 2007).

Given the situation in those territories, many states also said that there was an urgent need for more assistance to the liberation movements by the UN, specialised agencies, and the international community (UN YB, 1972). In that connection, several states referred to the resolution adopted at the ninth session of the Assembly of

Heads of State and Government of OAU, held in Rabat, Morocco, in June 1972, which called for increased assistance to the liberation movements (OAU, 1972).

Some states held that a peaceful solution to the question was still attainable and that efforts should be continued to bring about negotiations between the national liberation movements and Portugal (Ibid). The Secretary-General of PAIGC, Amilcar Cabral said that the Fourth Committee should consider the following proposals: representations to the Government of Portugal for the immediate start of negotiations between its representatives and those of the PAIGC; and immediate acceptance of PAIGC delegates, in the capacity of associate members or observers, in all the specialised agencies in the UN as the sole legitimate representatives of the people of Guinea; development of practical assistance from the specialised agencies to the people of Guinea; and moral and political support by the UN for initiatives of the people of Guinea and PAIGC, with a view of ending the Portuguese colonial war and achieving independence (Ibid)

The Vice-President of FRELIMO, Marcelino dos Santos expressed gratitude to those organisations and governments which had assisted his organisation and said that FRELIOMO was prepared to negotiate with Portugal on condition that it formerly recognise Mozambique's right to self-determination and independence (Ibid). It can be deduced from words such as 'prepared to negotiate' that only armed struggle was an answer to the solution to their problems, and such expresses also helped the world body (UN) push the colonial power to come to terms with the principles of self-determination and independence.

Further, in accordance with the Fourth Committee's decision, representatives of the SWAPO; ZAPU and ZANU participated in the Committee consideration of their territories in an observer capacity. The SWAPO was represented in the discussions of Secretary for External Affairs, Peter Mushihange and Theo-Ben Gurirab, the organisation's representative at the UN in New York, at the Fourth Committee's meetings, held on 6 and 11 December 1972, respectively (ORGA, 1972). Not only did participation of the leadership of the movements in the Committee, provide them with an opportunity to present their case before it, but also implied acknowledgement by the world community that they would become future heads of post-colonial countries.

The ZAPU was represented by Jane Ngwenya (Zimbabwe Review, 1975), a member of the National Executive Committee, and Aaron Ndlovu, a member of the Revolutionary Council; while the ZANU was represented by Richard Hove, Secretary for External Affairs. Both Jane Ngwenya and Richard Hove made statements before the Fourth Committee, at its meetings held on 10 December 1972 (ORGA, 1972).

Ngwenya expressed her gratitude to the UN and the Fourth Committee in particular, for enabling the representatives of liberation movements to appear as observers and thus, recognise the legitimacy of the armed liberation struggle as the only course open to the people of those countries still toiling under the colonial yoke (Ibid). Hove said, in ZANU's view, revolutionary violence was a legitimate response to reactionary; and that the Zimbabweans would have preferred to talk rather than to kill or be killed, but they had unfortunately been compelled to accept violence (Ibid).

Speaking on behalf of his organisation (SWAPO), Mushihange expressed profound appreciation for the Fourth Committee's decision to adopt the proposal of the Special Committee on the Situation regarding implementing the Declaration on the Granting of Independence to Colonial Countries and Peoples to grant observer status to the national liberation movements which were recognised by the OAU (ORGA, 1972). According to Mushihange, that decision was most prompt, since the universe was increasingly realising that the national liberation movements were the visible expression of the aspirations of the oppressed peoples of colonial Africa. For him, the OAU itself had decided at Rabat, Morocco in June 1972 to grant observer status to the national liberation movements (OAU, 1972) and that the Conference of Foreign Ministers of the Non-Aligned Countries had taken a similar position at Georgetown, Guyana in August 1972 (Stubbs, 2003). Therefore, Mushihange expressed on behalf of the SWAPO, Namibia's people's desire for freedom and independence, and reversed the right to speak during the debate on Namibia in the Fourth Committee (Ibid). As a general observation, and of course, considering the statements of the representatives of the liberation movements, granting an observer status implied that the movements were 'states in waiting', for they also conducted their own foreign relations matters.

On 14 December 1972, the Fourth Committee approved, based on the statement of the representative of SWAPO, a draft resolution on

Namibia. This resolution was adopted by the Assembly four days later. The GA recorded in the preambular paragraphs of the text that it had invited, in consultation with OAU, representatives of the national liberation movement of Namibia—the SWAPO—to participate in an observer capacity in the consideration of the territory and had heard the statement of a representative of the movement (A/RES 3031—XXVII, 1972).

Meanwhile, the Fourth Committee also approved two draft resolutions on Zimbabwe on 7 December 1972, based on the statements of the representatives of ZAPU and ZANU. GA adopted both texts concurrently (Ibid). By the operative part of the first resolution, the Assembly, among other things, requested all governments, the specialised agencies and other organisations concerned, in consultation with the OAU, to extend all moral and material assistance to the people of Zimbabwe (Ibid).

At its 1973 session, the GA as in 1972, on the recommendation of the Fourth Committee, and Special Political Committee, once again decided to grant observer status to the African liberation movements recognised by OAU. Thus, the following representatives of the OAU recognised liberation movements took part in the Fourth Committee discussions in an observer capacity relating to the territories under Portuguese administration: Mangali Tula, National Front for the Liberation of Angola (FNLA); and Sharfudine Khan, FRELIMO (UN YB, 1973).

On 12 October 1973, the Special Political Committee heard among others, statements from the representatives of South African liberation movements. Thereafter, the Special Committee Political Committee approved, based on those statements, by acclamation a draft resolution (ORGA, 1974), condemning the failure of the Government of South to comply with the repeated requests of the GA and SC for the release of all persons imprisoned and interned, or otherwise for their opposition to apartheid (Ibid).

Notably, South Africa's failure to comply with the Assembly and SC's repeated requests to release all persons imprisoned or interned resulted in an increased role of international assistance groups such as the International Defence and Aid Fund (IDAF) and the International Committee of the Red Cross (ICRC) as far as the liberation movements' struggle was concerned (Shepperd, 1974).

On 9 November 1973, the Fourth Committee approved, based on representative statements, two resolutions that the GA adopted three days later (UN YB, 1973). By the preamble of the first resolution, the Assembly reaffirmed that the Angolan and Mozambican national liberation movements were the authentic representatives of the true aspirations of the people of those territories (Ibid).

The GA recommended that pending their accession to independence, all governments, specialised agencies and other organisations within the UN system and the UN bodies concerned should, when dealing with matters regarding the territories, ensure their representation by the national liberation movements concerned in an appropriate capacity and consultation with OAU (Ibid). By implication, the GA had elevated the representatives of liberation movements to status of heads of government, even before they could be—a development which those representatives, hopefully, enjoyed.

Regarding Zimbabwe, it was Edward Ndlovu of ZAPU and Mukudzei Mudzi of ZANU who took part in an observer capacity during the Fourth Committee discussions on the territory. On 20 November, the Fourth Committee approved two draft resolutions, following a debate and considering representative statements, which the GA later adopted on 12 December 1973 (UN YB, 1973).

The Assembly reaffirmed in the operative part of the first text that there should be no independence before majority rule in Zimbabwe; and stated that any settlement relating to the future of the territory be worked out with the full participation of the genuine political leaders and representatives of the national liberation movements, who were the sole and authentic representatives of the true aspirations of the people of Zimbabwe (Ibid).

For Namibia, it was, among others, Veiue N Mbaeva and Mburumba Kerina, both representing the South West Africa National United Front (SWANUF), who participated in the Fourth Committee discussions. On 4 December 1973, the Fourth Committee approved a draft resolution, later adopted by the Assembly on December 12, recognising SWAPO as the authentic representative of the Namibian people, following discussions and representative statements. Therefore, the GA asked all states and organisations within the UN system, to render to the Namibian people [via SWAPO], in cooperation with the OAU, all moral and material assistance necessary to continue their struggle for freedom (UN YB, 1973).

As in the previous years, the Fourth Committee and the Special Political Committee invited the representatives of the liberation movements recognised by the OAU to take part as observers in the proceedings relating to Territories under Portuguese administration, Zimbabwe, Namibia and South Africa in 1974. The invitation for representatives of South African liberation movements was based on the OAU decision of 19 February 1973 requesting a Special Political Committee, to work closely with the ANC, headquartered in Morogoro, and the PAC headquartered in Dar es Salaam, Tanzania (UN YB, 1974).

Consequently, Mzwandile Piliso, a member of the National Executive of the ANC, and Potlako Leballo, Acting President of the PAC, participated in the Special Political Committee's meetings, as observers, on 21 March 1974 (GA OR, 1974). As for the representatives of the liberation movements from the territories under Portuguese administration to take part in the Fourth Committee discussions, the invitation was based on the GA decision of 3 October 1974 as recommended by the Committee, having been approved by its chairperson on 23 September (Ibid).

The invited representatives to take part in the Fourth Committee discussions/proceedings included Miguel Trovoada, Movement for the Liberation of Sao Tome, and Principe (MLSTP); Sharfudine M. Khan, FRELIMO; Mangali Tula, FNLA (Angola); Saydi Vifira Dias Mingas, Popular Movement for the Liberation of Angola (MPLA); and Abilio Monteiro Durate, PAIGC (UN YB, 1974).

During the discussion of the item, many speakers expressed satisfaction with Portugal's recognition of the right of self-determination and independence, emphasising that the national liberation movements of the territories in question had brought about the changes through their determined struggle for freedom. In general, most representatives shared the view that the process of decolonisation should continue without delay (Ibid).

On that basis, the Fourth Committee approved without objection a draft resolution on 11 December 1974. This resolution was adopted by the GA also without objection, on 13 December, as Resolution 3294—XXIX. In its preamble, the Assembly welcomed Portugal's declaration accepting its Charter obligations and recognising the right of self-determination and independence (A/RES 3294—XXIV, 1974).

The GA also recognised that the changes in Portugal's policy towards its colonial territories were brought about mainly because of the struggle and persistent resistance of the people of the territories led by their national liberation movements. It, therefore, recalled the responsibility of the UN to continue to render all moral and material aid to those peoples and the national liberation movements recognised by the OAU in their efforts to consolidate national unity and reconstruct their countries (Ibid).

Regarding Mozambique, the GA through its resolution, urged member states, (particularly developed countries) and UN organisations (particularly the financial institutions) to swiftly assist FRELIMO with the immediate and pressing economic and social problems stemming from the country's pre-independence situation. For Southern Rhodesia/Zimbabwe, the Fourth Committee invited Noel Mukono (ZANU) and T. George Silundika (ZAPU) and heard a statement by Reverend Canaan Banana, leader of the Zimbabwe African National Council (ANCZ), at the GA's twenty-ninth session in 1974 (Ibid).

During the debate in the Fourth Committee, many of the members saw that the United Kingdom (UK), as an administering authority should call for a constitutional conference in which the leaders of the ANCZ would play a major part. On that basis, the Fourth Committee approved two resolutions on the question of Zimbabwe, on 28 November 1974: one concerning the territory as a whole and the other relating to the question of sanctions. These texts were adopted by the GA also on 13 December 1974 (Ibid, 141).

By the operative part of the first resolution, the Assembly, among other things, reaffirmed that the national liberation movements of Zimbabwe were the sole and authentic representatives of their true aspirations; and that any settlement be worked out with the full participation of the genuine political leaders and leaders of the national liberation movements and be endorsed freely and fully by the Zimbabwean people (Ibid).

The Fourth Committee considered the issue of Namibia at its meetings held between 15 October and 29 November 1974. It invited three representatives of SWAPO: Theo-Ben Guriab, Peter Mushihange and John Ya Otto to take part in an observer capacity during its consideration of the question. It also heard statements by, among others, Gerson Veii of the South West African National Union

(SWANU), on the question of Namibia during those meetings. It considered the question at the meetings held between 15 October and 29 November 1974 (Ibid, 156).

Most speakers on the question of Namibia approved the growing political and military struggle undertaken by the Namibian people, and led by SWAPO, emphasising the need for continued armed struggle and advocating moral and material support for SWAPO which, they said, had become increasingly effective under the leadership of SWAPO; emphasised the need for the armed struggle to continue; and to provide SWAPO with moral and material support (Ibid, 157).

On 13 December 1974, the GA acting on the recommendation of the Fourth Committee, adopted without objection, a resolution which the Committee had unanimously approved, as revised by the sponsors, on 29 November. Under the resolution, the Assembly, among other things, noted with satisfaction the arrangements for the representation of the national liberation movements in the work of the Special Committee on the Granting of Independence to Colonial Countries and Peoples, the UN Council for Namibia, and the Fourth Committee. Therefore, it expressed its appreciation of the movements 'participation in the proceedings of those committees or organs (A/RES 3296—XXIX, 1974).

*2.2.2 Special Committee on the Granting of Independence to Colonial Countries and Peoples*

The Special Committee on the Granting of Independence to Colonial Countries and Peoples (Special Committee on Independence) was set up under Resolution 1654 (XVI) of 27 November 1961. Some believe that the Special Committee became one of the most active groups set up by the GA (Barber, 1975). Others, like Mittelman (1976), believe it served as a major international instrument of decolonisation. Members of the Special Committee were appointed by the President of the GA on 23 January 1962. They were Australia, Cambodia, Ethiopia, India, Italy, Madagascar, Mali, Poland, Syria, Tanganyika (Tanzania), Tunisia, USSR, the United Kingdom of Great Britain and Ireland, the USA, Uruguay, Venezuela, and Yugoslavia. This membership was subsequently, increased from seventeen to twenty-four (UN YB, 1962), hence the name UN Committee of 24.

The main task of the Special Committee was to examine the application of the 1960 Declaration on the Granting of Independence to Colonial countries and peoples, to make suggestions and recommendations on the progress and extent of the implementation of the Declaration and to report to the GA at its seventeenth session (A/RES 1654—XVI, 1961). Additionally, it was also authorised to meet outside UN Headquarters when necessary for effective functions, in consultation with the appropriate authorities (Ibid).

The Special Committee began its work on 20 February 1962. Most of the territories within the Special Committee's scope of competence were in Africa. These territories included, among others, in Africa; Southern Rhodesia/Zimbabwe, Angola, Mozambique and Namibia (UN YB, 1962).

On 1 March 1962, it agreed to receive written petitions and hearings of petitioners. However, by the end of the 1960s, the Special Committee had not achieved any considerable progress regarding processing the petitions. The main reason for the lack of progress was that the Special Committee did not have a criterion for granting hearings and distributing petitions as official documents (ORGA, 1962); and African diplomats' efforts to seek recognition of individual petitions and the colonial powers' tireless efforts to prevent those petitions (Burke, 2010).

On 20 December 1971, the GA endorsed the Special Committee's proposal, to take steps, in consultation with the OAU, to enable representatives of national liberation movements in the colonial territories in Southern Africa to participate, in an appropriate capacity, in its deliberations relating to those territories (A/RES2878—XXVI, 1971). The Special Committee's proposal was made in the context of the Assembly resolutions by which the Special Committee was directed to send visiting missions to colonial territories and to hold meetings at places where it could best obtain first-hand information on the situation in colonial territories (GA OR, 1974).

Following that arrangement, the Special Committee decided to send an Ad Hoc Group to Africa maintain contact with the representatives from national liberation movements (Ibid, 196). Headed by the Chairperson of the Special Committee, the Ad Hoc Group consisted of representatives of Bulgaria, Ethiopia, Sweden, Syria, Tanzania, and Venezuela. It visited the following capitals for approximately two to five working days, starting from 10 May 1971: Lusaka, Dar es Salaam and Addis Ababa (Ibid).

While in Africa, the Ad Hoc Group established contacts with the national liberation movements and heard statements by their representatives. As a rule, the Ad Hoc Group held its meetings in public, and those meetings conducted in private were held at the request of the representatives of the movements concerned (Ibid, 180).

In Lusaka (Zambia), the Ad Hoc Group met with Pascal Luvualu, member of the Central Committee [MPLA]; Nathan Shamuyarira, Secretary-General [ZANU]; Moses Garoeb, Administrative Secretary [SWAPO]; Ray E. Simons, member of the Executive Committee, South African Congress of Trade Unions [SACTU] (South Africa); G.B. Nyandoro [ZAPU]; Paulo J. Gumane, President [COREMO] and Miniban J. Ntundumula, member of COREMO (Ibid, 179). The Group also met with A. Fatar, Joint Secretary, Unity Movement of South Africa [UMSA]; Jane Cool, representative of UMSA in Lusaka; and Grielme Chippa, Captain of the National Union for Total Independence of Angola [UNITA] (Ibid).

In Dar es Salaam (Tanzania), the Ad Hoc Group met Duma Nokwe, Director of Political Affairs, ANC (South Africa); Joachim Chissano, Chief Representative, FRELIMO in Tanzania; and Sergio Vieira, Representative of FRELIMO in Egypt; Ahmed G. Ebrahim, Deputy Secretary for Foreign Affairs, PAC (South Africa); Andreas Chipanga, Acting Secretary for Information and Publicity [SWAPO]; Jesaya Nyamu, Information Officer of SWAPO; and Agostinho Neto, President of MPLA (Ibid, 180).

Concerning the question of Namibia, representative of SWAPO, among other things, empathetically rejected any plebiscites in the territory under the auspices of the Republic of South Africa (Ibid, 181). The representatives of FRELIMO and MPLA reported that their movements controlled approximately one-third of their territories and that where they had established a political and social structure to meet the needs of the people hitherto not met by the Portuguese colonialist authorities; and informed the Ad Hoc Group that information available to them indicated that the allies of Portugal were considering direct military intervention in Mozambique to buttress the Portuguese domination (Ibid, 182)).

Representative of the MPLA stated that the Cunene River Basin Project, although at that moment suspended, had the same sinister purpose as the Cabora Basa Dam Scheme, to which particular attention of the Special Committee should be drawn (Ibid). Given the worries about a possible spill-over of 'SWAPO terrorism' to the Portuguese side of the border, Portuguese officials also started to rethink the mechanisms of local rule in the Cunene region. That included, in the 1960s, a new effort to strengthen the prestige of the chiefs (Ibid).

Meanwhile, the representatives of two movements from South Africa, PAC, and the ANC repeated their strong call for the expulsion forthwith of South Africa and Portugal from the UN and all its agencies; and strongly appealed to the world body through the Ad Hoc Group to declare its full support of the people in colonial territories and deny the colonists and racists regimes the use of UN facilities for their propaganda (GA OR, 1974).

Representatives of the liberation movements from Zimbabwe stated that they believed no economic sanction against the illegal regime would be ineffective without extending to South Africa and Portugal and being enforced by force. They also informed the Ad Hoc Group of their dilemma regarding assistance from the UN High Commissioner for Refugee (UNHCR). In general, OAU-recognised national liberation movements generally urged the UN to grant them sole recognition as the legitimate representatives of the people in Southern Rhodesia/Zimbabwe, Angola, Mozambique, and Namibia (Ibid).

The Special Committee considered the report of the Ad Hoc Group, which also encompassed the preliminary oral report of the mission's Chairperson, on 10 April 1972. Among other things, the Chairman stated, in the report that the Special Committee believed its recognition of PAIGC as the *de facto* and the sole and authentic representative for the aspirations of the people of the territory should be taken fully into account by the States and by the agencies and other organisations within the UN system in dealing with matters relating to Guinea (Bissau) and Cape Verde UN YB, 1972).

On 13 April 1972, the Special Committee, based on the conclusions of the Mission, adopted a resolution relating to Guinea (Bissau) and Cape Verde. Among other things, it appealed to all States, the specialised agencies, and other organisations within the UN system, directly or indirectly or in consultation with the OAU, to render to the people of Guinea (Bissau) and Cape Verde, through their national liberation movement—PAIGC—all moral and material assistance necessary to continue their struggle for self-determination and independence (Ibid, 587).

On 20 April 1972, the Special Committee adopted another resolution relating to all the Portuguese-administered territories. In particular, the Committee expressed its appreciation for the renewed invitations extended to it by the MPLA and the FRELIMO to visit the liberated areas of Angola and Mozambique and asked its chairman to continue consultations with the OAU and with the liberation movements to work out the necessary modalities for the dispatch of a special mission to those territories (Ibid, 588).

Within the context of the GA resolution by which it was authorised to meet elsewhere than at Headquarters [New York City] in the discharge of its functions, the Special Committee held a series of meetings in Africa between 10 and 28 April 1972. The purpose of these meetings was to underscore the solidarity of the UN with the colonial peoples struggling for freedom and to enlarge the Committee's capacity to help those peoples realise in realising their aspirations (Ibid, 540).

During its meetings in Africa, the Special Committee heard statements from PAIGC (Guinea-Bissau) and Cape Verde representatives in Conakry. At Lusaka, the Special Committee heard representatives of the MPLA (Angola); COREMO and FRELIMO (Mozambique); ZAPU, ZANU and FROLIZI (Zimbabwe); SWAPO (Namibia); ANC and UMSA (South Africa). At Addis Ababa, it heard FNLA (Angola); SWANUF (Namibia); and the Movement for Liberation of Djibouti [MLD] [Djibouti] (GA OR, 1972).

On 28 August, the Special Committee, after discussion, decided to consider inviting, in consultation with the OAU and through it, the representatives of the liberation movements concerned to participate, whenever necessary and in an observer capacity, in its proceedings relating to their territories; and further decided to recommend to the Assembly that it make available the necessary funds for that purpose in 1973. The GA approved these recommendations on November 2, 1972, via GA Resolution 2908—XXVII.

In 1973, and as envisaged in its 1972 report to the GA, the Special Committee decided, in consultation with the OAU, again invited representatives of the national liberation movements of the colonial territories in Africa to take part as observers in its proceedings relating to their respective countries. The Special Committee, therefore, recommended that the Assembly continue with the arrangements concerning the participation of the liberation movements in question in its work during 1974, and of the Fourth Committee for that matter (UN YB, 1973).

In response, representatives of the ZAPU and ZANU (Zimbabwe); FNLA and MPLA (Angola); FRELIMO (Mozambique); SWAPO (Namibia); PAIGC (Guinea Bissau and Cape Verde); and Movement for Liberation of Comoros [MOLINCO] (Comoro Archipelago) took part as observers in the relevant proceedings of the Special Committee during 1973 (GA OR, 1975).

Together, those observers gave the Special Committee information on the situation in their territories, as well as the progress of the liberation struggle and the needs thereof (UN JYB, 1974). The SWAPO was represented by Petuse Norah Appolus, who made statements at the Special Committee's meetings, on 25 and 29 June, respectively (GA OR, 1975).T. George Silundika stood for the ZAPU, while ZANU was represented by S.V. Mtambanengwe, who made statements at the Special Committee meeting on 23 April (Ibid, 3).

Sasa Mbala (FNLA), Mesamesa Tshamba (MPLA), and Manuel Jorge (FRELIMO) all made statements before the Special Committee at its meetings held between 18 and 22 June (Ibid, 108). Marcelino dos Santos, Vice-President of FRELIMO, also participated in the Special Committee's proceedings regarding the massacre of villagers in Mozambique (Ibid).

Participating as an observer for the first time, Petuse Norah Appolus (SWAPO) stated that the Namibian people were determined to continue opposing the illegal South African regime in Namibia, which was forcing them into homelands and denying their fundamental human rights (ibid). At the same time, according to Appolus, the South African Government had flouted international public opinion by pretending that it was willing to negotiate seriously; and that dialogue with that Government should be ended (UN YB, 1973).

Mtambanengwe (ZANU), among other things, assured the Special Committee that the struggle for national liberation would continue until Zimbabwe was entirely liberated, and said that the intensity of the war had made the illegal regime utterly desperate and led it to employ brutal repressive measures against the African population (Ibid, 223-224).

Silundika (ZAPU), among other things, urged the Special Committee to recommend that action be taken against the countries and corporations, which were contravening sanctions and appealed for more effective international aid to the national liberation movements, which would consider the military repercussions being given to the illegal regime by South Africa (Ibid).

Together, the representatives of the FNLA, MPLA and the FRELIMO provided the Special Committee with information on new developments in their armed struggle and on progress made in national reconstruction in the liberated areas; and paid special tribute to Amilcar Cabral, leader of PAIGC who was assassinated on 20 January 1973 (Ibid, 741).

*2.2.3 UN Council for Namibia*

The UN Council for Namibia was established under the terms of the GA Resolution 2248—S-V of May 1967. First, it was the UN Council for South West Africa, and later in 1968 renamed the UN Council for Namibia, when the Assembly proclaimed that, following the wishes of its people, the Territory would be thenceforth known as Namibia (UNTAG, https://peacekeeping.un.org). The Council was created to function as the legal government of Namibia in international fora (Barrat, 1990). Its functions and powers were among other things, to transfer all powers to the people of Namibia upon the declaration of independence. In the exercise of its powers, the Council was accountable to the Assembly (A RES 2248—S-V, 1967).

Composed of Chile; Columbia; Guyana; India; Indonesia; Nigeria; Pakistan Turkey; United Arab Republic (Egypt); Yugoslavia; and Zambia, members of the UN Council for Namibia were elected by the GA on 13 January 1967 (Ibid). Since its start, the UN Council for Namibia has consulted with various Namibia groups. For instance, it reported to the twenty-seventh session of the GA saying that it was not able to resolve the question of the participation of Namibians in its work (OR GA, 1972).

Nevertheless, the Council was gratified that SWAPO's representative accepted the opportunity to attend Council meetings as an (Ibid). To also allow all Namibians, especially those who could not come to New York or who had no representatives there, the Council requested its Mission to consult with them or with their representatives during its visits to Europe and Africa (Ibid).

Subsequently, in Kenya and Istanbul, the mission met with Jackson Kambode, Foreign Secretary of the South West African United Front (SWANUF) and Charles Kauraisam the External Secretary, also representing Gerson Veii, President of SWANUF (Ibid). Based on the conclusions and recommendations of the Mission, the UN Council for Namibia also granted requests for hearings, among others, to Theo-Ben Gurirab of the SWAPO in January and Sam Nujoma in May 1972 (Ibid).

On 19 December 1972 and 7 May 1973, the Council heard Charles Kauraisa of SWANU. Kauraisa congratulated the Council on the position it had taken, particularly during the discussion of the question of Namibia in the SC; and stated, amongst other things, that his organisation (SWANU) had consistently stressed that the Council for Namibia should be properly constituted with a distinct administrative machinery and a permanent Commissioner to carry out executive and administrative tasks (GA OR, 1974).

In 1973, the Council conducted its mission in Africa and Europe and held a special session in Lusaka, Zambia. There, it met with leaders of SWAPO including its President Sam Nujoma and its Acting Secretary for Foreign Affairs, Peter Mweshinhanga, accompanied by Shohana Shikomba, Representative of SWAPO in East Africa and Simon Kankwanga, Director of SWAPO Elders (Ibid, 30). From 6 to 14 June 1973, the Council held a special session which was attended by a delegation of the Government of Zambia, led by E.H.K. Mudenda, Minister for Foreign Affairs. The SWAPO delegation, including Sam Nujoma, fully participated in the session as observers, with all delegations making statements (Ibid).

On 14 June, by a unanimous decision, the Council adopted the Lusaka Declaration on the UN Council for Namibia. It said, among other things: that it was incumbent on all nations to actively support the struggle of the Namibian people, both politically and materially including closer collaboration with SWAPO and close cooperation with the OAU (Ibid).

Following the Council's report, the GA in Resolution 3031—XXVII, requested the UN Council for Namibia, *inter alia*, to ensure the participation appropriate capacity of the Namibian people in its activities (RES 3031—XVIII, 1973). The Assembly also requested the Secretary-General to take effective steps, including increasing moral, political, and material assistance to the Namibian people and their liberation movement (Ibid).

Subsequently, the UN Council for Namibia reported to the twenty-eighty session of the GA that it had granted observer status to SWAPO, the OAU-recognised Namibian liberation movement. Thus, the representative of SWAPO in New York participated fully in all the meetings of the Council (GA OR, 1972). Accordingly, whenever the situation demanded, the delegation of SWAPO was led by its President, Sam Nujoma, who informed the Council of the significance of important developments affecting Namibia and took an active role in the Council's discussions and enlarged the membership of the Council to twenty-five (A/RES 3111—XXVIII, 1973).

Also, under Resolution 3111—XXVIII, the GA recognised that the national liberation movement of Namibia, SWAPO was the authentic representative of the Namibian people and supported the efforts of the movement to strengthen national unity; and called on all specialised agencies and other organisations within the UN system to take the necessary steps to enable the UN Council for Namibia, as the legal authority for the territory, to participate fully in the work of those agencies and organisations (Ibid). In addition, the Assembly decided to defray the expenses of a representative of the SWAPO when accompanying such missions as the UN Council for Namibia might determine and whenever called for consultation by the Council (Ibid).

By Resolution 3295—XXIX, the Assembly approved the report of the UN Council for Namibia: authorised adequate financial provision in the budget of the Council to finance an office for SWAPO in New York; and decided to defray the expenses of a representative of SWAPO when on any mission approved by the Council (A/RES 3295—XXIX, 1974). It also requested all inter-governmental and non-governmental organisations and conferences to, among other things, co-operate with the UN Council for Namibia and SWAPO in the elaboration of programmes for assistance to Namibians and programmes of dissemination of information; and all its committees and sub-committees to invite the representative of the UN Council for Namibia and of SWAPO to take part in their meetings whenever the rights and interests of Namibia were discussed (Ibid).

By its decision of 14 May 1974, the UN Council for Namibia had accepted the invitation to be represented at the OAU Council of Ministers' twenty-eighth ordinary session to be held at Mogadishu, Somalia, from 6 to 11 June 1974. On 6 June, after hearing the opening address by the President of the Revolutionary Council of Somalia, Mohamad Jaalle Siyad Barre, the Council of Ministers elected its officers, adopted its agenda, and referred the question of Namibia to its political committee for consideration (GA OR, 1975).

During the discussion of the question of Namibia, Sam Nujoma, the President of SWAPO issued an aide memoire. Nujoma stated that the Security Council's unanimous adoption of Resolution 342 (1973) on December 11, 1973, was the culmination of SWAPO's consistent efforts, support of the OAU. This resolution aimed to end "contacts" between the UN Secretary-General and the South African government, as SWAPO firmly believed these contacts were futile and South Africa was insincere. In all that, Nujoma said they would like and were requesting the OAU to take the initiative by having its Member States request the SC to convene as soon as possible and to consider enforcement measures under Chapter VII of the Charter (Ibid).

Through the Council, SWAPO was also able to take part in the work of the various bodies in which the Council itself had representation. These bodies included, among others: the United Nations High Commission for Refugees (UNHCR); the United Nations Education, Scientific and Cultural Organisation (UNESCO); the World Health Organisation (WHO), the United Nations Children's Emergency Fund (UNICEF); and the Food and Agricultural Organisation [FAO] (GA OR, 1974). In practice, representatives of the SWAPO had taken part fully, in an observer capacity, in the meetings of the UN Council for Namibia since 1972 and continued to do so, until the independence of Namibia in 1990.

*2.2.4 UN Economic Commission for Africa*

Headquartered in Addis Ababa, Ethiopia, the Economic Commission for Africa (ECA) was set up in 1958 under Resolution 671A—XXV of the ECOSOC. In the exercise of its power, the ECOSOC, not only set up the ECA but also prescribed the legal framework concerning its functions and membership. This legal framework was referred to in the resolution that set up the Commission as 'the Terms of Reference of the ECA' (ECOSOC RES 671 A—XXV, 1958).

The framework provided that the ECA's functions, performed within the UN framework, were subject to ECOSOC's general supervision and required the agreement of any country before acting (Akiwumi, 1972). In particular, the function of the ECA was to initiate and participate in measures for facilitating concerted action for the economic and social development of Africa to raise the level of activity and levels of living standard in Africa, and for maintaining and strengthening economic relations of the countries and territories of Africa both among themselves and with other countries of the world (Ibid).

As a regional organisation, the Commission covered the whole continent of Africa, Madagascar, and other African Islands, e.g., Mauritius. Its membership was of two kinds, full and associate. All independent states of Africa were full members with voting rights, also those metropolitan countries, like the United Kingdom (UK) and France, with territorial and colonial responsibilities in Africa; however, these ceased to be members once they relinquished any such responsibilities. Associate members, typically non-self-governing territories, could fully participate in Commission debates and discussions, but lacked voting rights (Chidzero, 1963).

The ECA had a membership of thirty-seven (37) members and seven associate members. Members of the UN, not members of the Commission, could attend the sessions of the Commission as observers, also UN specialised agencies, international organisations like the International Confederation of Free Trade Unions (ICFTU) or similar bodies (Ibid).

Since its establishment, the ECA has annually reported to the GA via ECOSOC on its activities and plans, including those of its subsidiary bodies. In 1963, for instance, the ECOSOC reconsidered its decision on the recommendation of the ECA in respect of the membership of Portugal and South Africa in the Commission. By this decision, the Council had rejected the suspension of Portugal and South Africa's membership from the ECA (ECOSOC, 1963). ECOSOC rejected their suspension because it was evident from the attitude already expressed by its members that it was not expected to take radical action and that other members raised the question of interference in the domestic affairs of certain states (Ibid).

After debating the membership issue, the ECOSOC adopted a draft resolution by which it decided to transmit the recommendations of the ECA to the GA. Subsequently, in Resolution 974 D (IV) of 30 July 1963, the Council decided to expel Portugal from the membership of the ECA and to suspend South Africa from participating in the work of the Commission (ECOSOC, RES 974 D—IV, 1963). Thereafter, a question arose as to how the non-self-governing territories of Angola, Mozambique, Guinea-Bissau and Namibia being associate members of the ECA should be represented in the Commission and who should designate such representatives (UN JYB, 1974).

Following consideration by the ECOSOC, and by successive sessions of the ECA, the Commission recommended in 1969 concerning associate membership for Angola, Mozambique, Guinea-Bissau and Namibia 'that the OAU should propose the names of representatives of the peoples of the countries in question and inform the Executive Secretary [of the ECA] accordingly to enable him to bring the matter before the GA. Based on this recommendation, the OAU in November 1970, proposed the names of persons to stand for the territories in question, those persons in each case the President or a senior office holder of the liberation movement recognised by the OAU (ECOSOC, 1971).

The proposed representatives of Angola, Guinea-Bissau and Mozambique on the ECA were: Agostinho Neto, President of MPLA (Congo Brazzaville, People's Republic of the Congo); Roberto Holden President of the FNLA (Kinshasa, Democratic Republic of the Congo); Amilcar Cabral Secretary-General of the PAIGC (Conakry, Guinea); and Marcelino Dos Santos Vice-President in Charge of External Relations of the FRELIMO (Dar es Salaam, United Republic of Tanzania). Sam Nujoma, SWAPO President, was added to the proposed OAU representatives list at the Tenth Council of Ministers Session in Tunis, 8-13 February 1971 (Ibid).

The participation for the time, of the representatives of Guinea (Bissau), Mozambique and Namibia in the work of the ECA was welcomed by the OAU Conference of Ministers (ECOSOC, 1971). On that basis, the Conference requested the Executive Secretary [of the ECA] to do everything in his power to assist the liberation movements of African countries under colonial domination, in their preparation for accession to national sovereignty in the best possible conditions by providing them with the means for training competent senior officials (Ibid). Following practice, the proposed representation required the approval of the GA. As for the case of Angola, Mozambique, and Guinea (Bissau), the names of the proposed representatives were duly submitted to the Assembly which expressly approved in terms of Resolution 2795—XXVI of 10 December 1971.

Based on the foregoing, the GA affirmed that the Angolan, Mozambican, Guinea-Bissau and Cape Verde national liberation movements were the sole legitimate representative of the people of those territories. It, therefore, recommended that, pending the accession of those Territories to independence, all Governments, the specialised agencies and other organisations within the UN system and UN bodies concerned should when dealing with matters about the Territories, ensure their representation by the liberation concerned in an appropriate capacity and consultation with the OAU (RES 2918—XXVII, 1972).

In the case of Namibia, the GA had delegated authority to the UN Council for Namibia to administer South West Africa until independence and to exercise other governmental functions, in accordance with Resolution 2248 (S-V). It, therefore, followed that the UN Council for Namibia was the appropriate body to approve arrangements for the representation of the Territory in the ECA. Accordingly, the name of the proposed representative was submitted to the Council, which approved the nomination at its 98th meeting held on 22 January 1971 (GA OR, 1972).

Initially, it was understood that the Namibian representative would act as SWAPO's President, expressing the views of the Namibian people at ECA meetings, rather than representing the Council for Namibia. Thus, in 1971, SWAPO's President Sam Nujoma's name was added to the list of the OAU proposed representatives (already mentioned).

In reporting to the Fifth Session of the ECOSOC, the ECA referred to the approval by the GA of the representation of Angola, Mozambique, and Guinea (Bissau), contained in the Assembly Resolution 2795—XXVI (already referred to), and to the approval by the UN Council for Namibia, at its 98th meeting, of the Namibian representative.

On that basis, the Commission reported that the representatives of Angola, Guinea-Bissau, Mozambique, and Namibia were invited to participate in the Commission as associate members; and that they had been invited to the third meeting of the Technical Committee of Experts held in Addis Ababa, Ethiopia in September 1972 (ECOSOC, 1973).

Following the ECA Resolution 233—X of 13 February 1971 on the participation of Angola, Guinea-Bissau, Mozambique, and Namibia in the work of the Commission, the Executive Secretary discussed with the representatives of the territories who attended the third meeting of the Technical Committee of Experts the assistance that the Commission could provide to the peoples of those territories (Ibid).

Therefore, it is seen that since 1971, Angola, Guinea-Bissau, Mozambique, and Namibia have been represented in the ECA through the President, Vice-President, or Secretary-General of their respective national liberation movements, recognised by the OAU. Except in the case of Guinea-Bissau, following its accession as the Republic of Guinea-Bissau (in 1973), the representation of the other territories remained in effect until independence. These were Angola, Mozambique; Zimbabwe; Namibia; and South Africa (Ibid).

The independence of Guinea-Bissau came as a result of claims that Portugal was no longer capable of ruling over most of the territory. Accordingly, since 1968, Amilcar Cabral, the PAIGC leader had started to contemplate unilateral a proclamation of independence as part of his strategy to win the war against the Portuguese—an issue that was postponed several times. It only came to fruition in the 1970s following recognition by the UN of the PAIGC as the sole and authentic representative population. The PAIGC held elections to the People's National Assembly and established the Republic of Guinea-Bissau on 24 September 1973 (Houser, 1973).

## *2.3 Conclusion*

This chapter's focus was on the practice of representation of national liberation at the UN. As noted, there were no pertinent rules and procedures for representation of national liberation movements in the UN, during its formative years. It is revealed, in the chapter that those rules and procedures evolved out of the authorising decisions of the GA and ECOSOC. As illustrated, the practice was that liberation movement representatives were invited through the OAU, with invitations transmitted by the Secretary-General after approval by the relevant UN General Assembly body or committee. As noted, such practice arose primarily from the UN GA organs or committees—the Fourth Committee of the GA; the Special Committee on Independence; the UN Council for Namibia and the ECA. As seen, the FRELIMO; ZAPU and ZANU; MPLA and FNLA; SWAPO; and ANC and PAC, took part in those committees and organs according to the UN practice. The following chapter discusses reactions and responses to the representation of national liberation movements at the UN.

# CHAPTER THREE

# UN Reactions and Responses to the Representation of National Liberation Movements

## 3.1 Introduction

This chapter is divided into three sections. The first section introduces the subject of UN reactions and responses to the representation of national liberation movements. The next section will outline the UN's reactions and responses, specifically detailing GA decisions adopted between 1965 and 1974. The last section concludes the chapter by providing a summary and highlights relating to how the UN came to play closer to the national liberation movements by adopting decisions, which pushed the movements higher on the political ladder.

When the UN was formed, national liberation movements were not regarded as equal stakeholders with the sovereign States in international institutions. This was because they fell within the authority of the administering powers. Later, considering the wave of African independence in 1960, they were given an international political platform to deliberate on the future of their countries alongside the primary lawmakers (States) in the UN. The association of national liberation movements with the UN resulted in independence and freedom for the people in colonial countries. After 1960, for example, the increasing African representation in the UN enlarged the GA, thereby making the region the largest bloc in the UN (O'Sullivan, 2005).

However, it must be noted that several factors mediated the results of the struggles for self-determination, independence, and freedom in Africa. The struggles for self-determination and independence were influenced by various factors: colonial education, churches, Pan-African support, exposure to the World Wars, and the forums provided by the League of Nations and later by the UN (Shimiyu, 1997).

Arguably, the UN has, over the years, acknowledged the role of national liberation movements in decolonisation (El-Ayouty, 1972). This was significant because it established the movements' international legal personality irreversibly (Brolman, 2007). It was expressed through the UN GA's decisions that offered international aid and support to the liberation movements (El-Ayouty, 1972). Others observe that it was expressed when the UN resolved, in cooperation with the OAU, to invite as observers regularly, the representatives of national liberation movements recognised by the OAU to participate in the relevant work of the Main Committees of the GA and its subsidiary organs, as well as conferences, seminars and other meetings held under the auspices of the UN which related to their countries (Shaw, 1983).

The acknowledgement of the role was also expressed when the GA requested the Secretary-General, Kurt Waldheim (of Germany) in consultation with the OAU, to ensure that the necessary arrangements were made for the liberation movements' effective participation, including the requisite financial provisions (Shaw, 1983).

It appears the UN established a pattern regarding its acknowledgment of the role of liberation movements in decolonisation. This is a pattern that is obscured and, therefore, creates a lacuna in the historiography of the African region.

An important starting point for understanding the UN's recognition of the role of national liberation movements in decolonisation is examining the GA's decisions on aid and support for the movements. This is especially true for those that were adopted during the period between 1965 and 1974. An analysis of these decisions is critical because they had a significant political impact (Martin-Bosch, 1987). Also, analysing the decisions is critical because they serve as a core of concentration in several significant ways. For example, they made the UN GA both the political pivot and the institutional pith of the entire UN system. In addition, examining these decisions is critical because they legitimised the African wars of national liberation and revealed recognition by UN bodies that the struggle against colonialism and apartheid in Southern Africa was a legitimate attempt as far as principles of the UN Charter and other UN declarations were concerned (El-Ayouty, 192)

## 3.2 The GA decisions on acknowledging the role of liberation movements in decolonisation

At its twentieth session, on 20 December 1965, the GA adopted Resolution 2105—XX. It envisaged the legality of petitions by the inhabitants of the territories inhabited by a people as defined under general international law. This law provided that all peoples inhabiting those territories and colonies were entitled to be enabled by administering States to freely and without interference from any quarter, to exercise their inalienable and universal right to self-determination. Accordingly, failure to implement this law gave people the right, including using armed struggle, to fight for independence as a last resort (Ya Nangoloh, 2013).

Adopted on the recommendation of the Special Committee on Independence, Resolution 2105—XX had 23 sponsors, namely, Afghanistan, Algeria, Burundi, Ceylon, Ethiopia, Ghana, Guinea, India, Iraq, Ivory Coast, Kenya, Mali, Mauritania, Nigeria, Rwanda, Sierra Leone, Somalia, Tunisia, Uganda, United Arab Republic (Egypt), Tanzania, Yemen and Yugoslavia. It was approved by the Assembly by a roll-call vote of 74 to 6, with 27 abstentions (UN YB, 1965).

The resolution marked a fundamental shift whereby the principle of self-determination was admitted to constituting a rule of international law, not a mere moral precept even though the UN was not able to specify the precise content of the right (Okudnag, 1971). For national liberation movements, in particular, the resolution was the first step towards victory in their struggle, because it gave them a *locus standi* in international law and relations (Olalia, 2006). This was generally an expression of satisfaction by the liberation movements as far as actions of the UN were concerned.

Under Resolution 2105—XX, the GA, requested the Special Committee on Independence: to continue to perform its task and to continue to seek the most effective means for the immediate and full application of the Declaration on Independence to all Territories (in Africa), which have not yet attained independence; and to pay particular attention to the small Territories and to recommend to the GA the most appropriate ways, as well as the steps to be taken, to enable the populations of those Territories to exercise fully their right to self-determination and independence (A/RES 2105—XX, 1965).

The Assembly also requested the Special Committee on Independence, whenever it considered it appropriate, to recommend a deadline for the accession to independence of each Territory by the wishes of the people; and recognise the colonial peoples' struggle by the peoples under colonial rule to exercise their right to self-determination and independence; and invited all States to provide material and moral assistance to the national liberation movements in colonial territories (Ibid).

In 1966, the GA took a step further with the adoption of Resolution 2189—XXI. Sponsored in the Fourth Committee by twenty-six powers, this resolution was adopted by a roll-call vote of 76 to 7, with twenty abstentions (UN YB, 1966). Significantly, the voting on Resolution 2189—XXI illustrated the world body's determination to support the national liberation movements' struggle against colonialism and apartheid in Southern Africa; and further, widened the gap between the UN and the colonial powers—South Africa, Portugal, and the UK, whose policies came to be viewed as a threat to international peace and security, especially as the trio voted against the text (El-Ayouty, 1972).

Under Resolution 2189—XXI, the Assembly recognised the legitimacy of the struggle of colonised peoples for self-determination and independence, inviting all states to provide material and moral assistance to national liberation movements. It further confirmed that the liberation process was irresistible and irreversible, legitimising the colonised people's resort to arms if colonial powers continued to oppose their aspirations (A/RES 2189—XXI, 1966).

In support of the provisions stipulated above, the GA declared that the preservation of colonialism and its manifestations, including racism and apartheid as well as colonial powers' attempts to suppress national liberation movements were incompatible with the UN Charter and the Declaration on Independence; and that the continuation of colonial rule threatened international peace and security and that the practice of apartheid, and racial discrimination, constituted a crime against humanity, and urged all States to provide moral and material assistance to the national liberation movements (Ibid).

The GA followed up with Resolution 2326—XXVII of 16 December 1967, adding more pressure on the colonial powers. Sponsored in the Fourth Committee by 20 powers, the resolution was adopted in the Assembly by 86 votes to 6, with 17 abstentions (UN

YB, 1967). Under this resolution, the Assembly reiterated that the persistence of colonialism and the suppression and the use of armed force against colonial peoples were incompatible with the Charter and the Declaration of Independence (A/RES 2326—XXVII, 1967).

The Assembly added that those issues also contravened the Universal Declaration on Human Rights. The GA continued 'that the practice of using mercenaries against movements for national liberation self-determination and independence was a punishable criminal act' and pointed out that the mercenaries themselves were outlaws (Ibid).

Therefore, it appealed to the Governments of all countries to enact legislation prohibiting the recruitment, financing, and training of mercenaries; and requested the colonial powers to dismantle their military bases and installations in the colonial territories and refrain from establishing new ones and from using those that still existed to interfere with the liberation of the peoples in those territories in the exercise of their legitimate right to freedom and independence (Ibid).

In 1968, the Assembly adopted a further decision reflecting the growing international recognition of the national liberation movements. This was in the form of Resolution 2465 (XXIII) adopted on 13 December 1968, by a roll-call vote of 79 to 5, with 19 abstentions (UN YB, 1968).

Under Resolution 2465—XXIII, the GA, among other things, reiterated its declaration that the practice of using mercenaries against movements for national liberation self-determination, and independence was a punishable criminal act; and reaffirmed its recognition of the legitimacy of the struggle of the colonial peoples to exercise their right to self-determination and independence (A/RES 2465—XXVIII, 1968).

The Assembly, also noted with satisfaction the progress made in the colonial territories by the national liberation movements, both through their struggle and through reconstruction programmes and urged all States to provide moral and material assistance to them; and appealed to all those States to comply with the provisions of its various resolutions and the SC concerning the colonial Territories, and in particular to give the necessary moral, political and material support to the people of the of those Territories in their legitimate struggles to achieve freedom and independence (Ibid).

On 11 December 1969, the GA took a series of decisions on the implementation of the Declaration of Independence. Thereby, the Assembly, among other things, reaffirmed again its recognition of the legitimacy of the struggle of the colonial peoples to exercise their right to self-determination and independence (Ibid). The GA, therefore, noted with satisfaction the progress made in the colonial Territories by the national liberation movements, both through their struggle and through reconstruction programs, and urged all States to provide moral and material aid to them (Ibid).

To further, support the actions of the national liberation movements, the Assembly repeated its call against the practice of using mercenaries against the movements. It was reiterated that mercenary activity is a punishable criminal act, and mercenaries are outlaws. Governments were urged to enact legislation criminalising the recruitment, financing, and training of mercenaries within their borders and to prohibit their nationals from serving as mercenaries (Ibid).

Further, the GA invited the Special Committee on Independence to continue to pay particular attention to the small territories and to recommend to the Assembly the most appropriate methods and steps to be taken to enable the populations of those territories to exercise fully their right to self-determination and independence; and also urged the administering powers to cooperate fully with the Special Committee by permitting visiting missions to the colonial territories to obtain first-hand information and to ascertain the wishes and aspirations of the inhabitants (Ibid).

Finally, the Assembly, requested Secretary-General, U. Thant (from Bruma), as suggested by the Special Committee on Independence to take concrete measures through all the media at his disposal, including publication, radio, and television to publicise the UN work in the field of decolonisation; and urged him, to give widespread of that work, especially that the continuing struggle for liberation being waged by the colonial peoples. Therefore, it requested the Member States to cooperate with the Secretary-General in promoting the large-scale dissemination of that information (Ibid).

Those decisions were taken in adopting Resolution 2465—XXIV, by 78 votes to 5, with 16 abstentions. Resolution 2465—XXIV had 20 sponsors, namely, Afghanistan, Algeria, Burundi, Ethiopia, India, Indonesia, Iraq, Mali, Mauritania, Nigeria, Pakistan, Sierra Leone,

Southern Yemen, Sudan, Syria, United Arab Republic (Egypt), Tanzania, Yemen, Yugoslavia, and Zambia (UN YB, 1969).

Also, in 1969, in pursuance of GA Resolution 2426—XXVIII of 18 December 1968, the Special Committee on Independence endorsed the report of its chairman's consultation with the President of the ECOSOC on the implementation of the Declaration by specialised agencies and international institutions (Ibid). The Special Committee on Independence thereby, recommended that those agencies and institutions, as well as the various programs within the UN system, take measures to increase the scope of their assistance to refugees from the colonial territories, particularly in Africa. It also recommended that those bodies give all possible assistance to the people struggling to liberate themselves from colonial rule, and, in particular, that they work out within the scope of their respective activities and in cooperation with OAU and through it with the national liberation movements, concrete programmes for assisting the people of Southern Rhodesia, Namibia and the territories under Portuguese administration (Ibid).

The Special Committee, therefore, appealed to the specialised agencies and the international institutions concerned to withhold from the Governments of Portugal and South Africa financial, economic, technical, and other assistance until they renounced their policies of racial discrimination and colonial domination. These decisions were embodied in a resolution adopted by the GA, on 2 October 1969 by a roll-call vote of 13 to 0, with 5 abstentions (Italy, the Ivory Coast, Norway, the UK, and the USA). The resolution was sponsored in the Assembly by the following members: Afghanistan; Bulgaria; India; Mali; and Tanzania (Ibid).

Meanwhile, at its mid-1969 session, the ECOSOC had considered the implementation of the Declaration by specialised and international institutions. Following the discussion, the Council, recommended among other things, to the specialised agencies and international institutions concerned that they establish relationship agreements and other special arrangements with OAU, as UNESCO had done, to give concrete assistance to the liberation movements to bring about a fuller and speedier implementation of the GA's decision thereon (Ibid, 636).

The ECOSOC also recommended that the UN (particularly the Office of Technical Cooperation), specialised agencies, and the international institutions (including UNDP and UNICEF) cooperatively and individually increase assistance to refugees from colonial territories, particularly in Africa. This included aid to relevant governments for preparing and executing projects beneficial to those refugees (Ibid, 638).

In addition, the ECOSOC urged the specialised agencies and international institutions concerned to introduce the greatest measure of flexibility into the procedures followed by them in the field of assistance to refugees from colonial territories, particularly in Africa, and to strengthen the existing arrangements for inter-agency cooperation to facilitate the planning and implementation of joint or complementary measures as well as, a concerted effort to address issues in the field (Ibid).

Those decisions were contained in ECOSOC Resolution 1450—XLVII, adopted on 7 August 1969, by a roll-call vote of 17 to 0), with 9 abstentions. Co-sponsored orally by Bulgaria, Resolution 1450—XLVII was adopted on the proposal of Bulgaria, Chad, Congo (Brazzaville), India, Kuwait, Libya, Sierra Leone, Sudan, Tanzania, and Upper Volta. The voting on the resolution was as follows: In favour: Bulgaria, Chad, Congo (Brazzaville), Guatemala, India, Indonesia, Jamaica, Kuwait, Libya, Mexico, Sierra Leone, Sudan, Tanzania, USSR, Upper Volta, Uruguay, Yugoslavia. Against: none. Abstaining: Argentina, Belgium, France, Ireland, Japan, Norway, Turkey, UK, USA (Ibid, 650).

On 12 October 1970, at its 1862nd plenary meeting, the GA adopted Resolution 2621 (XXV). The resolution was adopted by the Assembly with a recorded vote of 86 to 5, with fifteen abstentions. Resolution 2621 (XXVI set forth the programme for the full implementation of the Declaration on Decolonisation/Independence (UN YB, 1970). The resolution resulted in the liberation movements' occupation of a strategic ladder from which to operate, that is working from within the UN system like all other member States (Cristescu, 1981).

For the Portuguese-administered territories, the resolution was instrumental in the national liberation movements' diplomatic strategy. In general, the resolution represented the development of the UN anti-colonial thesis (Ibid). The Programme of Action confirmed the inherent right of colonial peoples to struggle by all necessary means at their disposal against colonial powers, which suppressed their aspiration for freedom and independence (Santos, 2012).

Under the operative part of the resolution, the Assembly declared that the further continuation of colonialism in all its forms and manifestations constituted a crime that constituted a violation of the UN Charter, the Declaration on Independence, and the principles of international law (A/RES 2621—XXV, 1970).

The GA also reaffirmed the inherent right of colonial peoples to struggle by all necessary means at their disposal against colonial powers that suppressed their aspiration for freedom and independence; and adopted a programme of action to assist in the full implementation of the Declaration on Independence (Ibid).

Therefore, it recommended that the representatives of liberation movements should be invited, whenever necessary, by the UN and other international organisations within the UN. Accordingly, that would enable the liberation movements to participate in an appropriate capacity in the proceedings of those organs relating to their countries (Ibid).

The proposed programme of action provided, among other things, that the member States should render all necessary moral and material assistance to the peoples of the colonial territories in their struggle to obtain freedom and independence; and that all freedom fighters under detention should be treated by the relevant provisions of the Geneva Convention relative to the Treatment of Prisoners of War; and, further, provided that representatives of liberation movements should be invited, whenever necessary, by the UN and other international organisations within the UN system to participate in an appropriate capacity in the proceedings of those organs relating to their countries (Ibid).

On 24 October 1970, on the Twenty-Fifth Anniversary of the UN, the GA adopted without a vote Resolution 2627 (XXV)—Declaration on the Twenty-fifth Anniversary of the UN. In Resolution 2627—XXV, the member states recognised the role of the UN in the past twenty-five years in the process of the liberation of peoples of colonial, Trust, and other Non-Self-Governing Territories (A/RES 2627—XXV, 1970). Because of that, the members said they welcomed the development wherein the number of sovereign states in the Organisation [UN] had been greatly increased and that the colonial empires had virtually disappeared (UN YB, 1970).

Despite those achievements, the members further claimed that many Territories and peoples continued to be denied their right to self-determination and independence, particularly in Namibia, Zimbabwe, Angola, Mozambique, and Guinea (Bissau), in deliberate and deplorable defiance of the UN and world opinion by certain recalcitrant States and by the illegal regime of Southern Rhodesia (Ibid).

Therefore, the members reaffirmed the inalienable right of all colonial peoples to self-determination, freedom, and independence, condemning all actions that denied these rights. They also recognised the legitimacy of colonial peoples' struggles for freedom by all appropriate means (Ibid)

Also, the same resolution called upon all governments to comply in that respect with the provisions of the Charter, taking into account the 1960 Declaration on the Granting of Independence; and re-emphasised that those countries and peoples were entitled, in their just struggle, to seek and to receive all necessary moral and material help by the purposes and principles of the Charter (A/RES 2627—XXV, 1970).

By Resolution 2704 (XXV) of 14 December 1970, the GA urged the UN specialised agencies and organisations concerned to take actions required for the full implementation of the relevant resolutions relating to the assistance of the national liberation movements and to discontinue all collaboration with the governments of Portugal, South Africa and the racist minority regime in Zimbabwe (A/RES 2704—XXV, 1970).

The Assembly, further, recommended that the specialised agencies and other organisations within the UN system, including in particular the United Nations Development Programme (UNDP) and the International Bank for Reconstruction and Development (IBRD), review all within their respective spheres of competence to increase the scope of their assistance to refugees from colonial territories (Ibid).

The GA Resolution 2704—XXV was adopted by eighty-three votes to four, with twenty-one abstentions, on the recommendation of the Fourth Committee. Its passing revealed the Assembly's support of the OAU's decisions concerning the resolution of the continent's conflicts and Africa's position thereof, and of course, the reason it decided to give material assistance to the national liberation movements (Biswaro, 2012). Resolution 2704—XXV ended UN specialised agencies' collaboration with Portugal and South Africa, allowing for invitations to African liberation movement leaders to agency meetings and offering assistance to those 'struggling for freedom from their colonial rule' (Duncan, 2004).

In Resolution 2708—XXV, the GA reiterated its conviction that the continuation of colonialism in all its forms, and manifestations and the attempts to suppress national liberation movements, were incompatible with the UN Charter, the Declaration, and the Universal Declaration of Human Rights, and posed a threat to global peace and security; and urged all States, the specialised agencies and other organisations within the UN system to provide, in consultation with the OAU, moral and material assistance to the national liberation movements in the territories (A/RES 2708—XXV, 1970).

The Assembly further reaffirmed its recognition of the legitimacy of the struggle of the colonial peoples and peoples under alien domination to exercise their right to self-determination and independence by all the necessary means at their disposal and noted with satisfaction the progress made in the colonial territories by the national liberation movements, both through their struggle and through reconstruction programs. The GA, therefore, urged all states, specialised agencies, and other organisations within the UN system to provide, in consultation, as appropriate, with the OAU, moral and material assistance to national liberation movements in the colonial territories (Ibid).

Resolution 2708—XXV was adopted by a roll-call vote of 93 to 5, with 22 abstentions. Its sponsors were: Algeria, Burundi, the Central African Republic, the Democratic Republic of the Congo, Ethiopia, Ghana, India, Indonesia, Iraq, Kenya, Liberia, Libya, Mali, Mauritania, Morocco, Nigeria, Pakistan, the People's Democratic Republic of Yemen, Senegal, Sierra Leone, Somalia, Sudan, Syria, Tunisia, Uganda, the United Arab Republic, the United Republic of Tanzania, Yemen, Yugoslavia, and Zambia (UN YB, 1970).

In effect, Resolution 2708—XXV legitimised all forms of resistance - including violence - in the struggle for self-determination—thereby legitimising the struggles of national movements if not always their practice methods (Dunning, 2016). The acceptance of the resolution also sanctioned the use by force of national liberation movements without stating it explicitly and expanded their right to use force in their struggles for self-determination (Salim, https://tamilnation.org).

Under Resolution 2787—XXVI of 6 December 1971, the GA expressed: concern 'that some countries, such as Portugal, with the support of the North Atlantic Treaty Organisation (NATO) allies, waged war against the national liberation movements of the colonies and certain independent States of Africa and Asia, including developing countries; and affirmed that the future of Zimbabwe could not be negotiated with an illegal regime and that any settlement had to be based on the 'no independence before majority rule' principle (A/RES 2787—XXVI, 1971).

The Assembly also reaffirmed the inalienable rights of all societies and in particular those of Zimbabwe, Namibia, Angola, Mozambique, Guinea-Bissau, and the Palestinian inhabitants, to freedom, equality, and self-determination, and by, the Declaration on the Principle of International Law Concerning Friendly Relations and Cooperation amongst States (Ibid).

Further, the GA, condemned the policies of certain NATO members that contributed to the creation of a military-industrial complex in Southern Africa, aimed at suppressing the movements of inhabitants, struggling for self-determination, and interfering in the affairs of independent African States (Ibid).

The GA Resolution 2787—XXVI was adopted by seventy-six votes to ten, with thirty-three abstentions, on the recommendation of the Third Committee (UN YB, 1971). This resolution confirmed the legality of instances of struggles for self-determination and national independence in Zimbabwe, Namibia, Angola, Mozambique, Guinea-Bissau, and the 'Palestine people (Higgins, 2004).

Under Resolution 2795—XXVI of 10 December 1971, the GA had approved the UN Economic Commission of Africa (ECA)'s arrangements made in consultation with the OAU, whereby, Angola, Mozambique, and Guinea-Bissau in their capacity as associate members of the ECA would be represented by their respective liberation movements (A/RES 2795—XXVI, 1971).

With the Assembly's approval of the ECA's arrangements, representatives from Angola (Agostino Neto for MPLA, Holden Roberto for FNLA), Mozambique (Marcelino dos Santos for FRELIMO), and Namibia (Sam Nujoma for SWAPO) attended the Tenth Session of the ECA (first Council of Ministers meeting) in Tunis in February 1971 as observers (ECOSOC, 1971).

Also, in Resolution 2795—XXVI, the GA further appealed to all States and the specialised agencies and other organisations within the UN system, in consultation with the OAU, to render to the peoples of the territories under Portuguese domination, in particular, the population in the liberated areas of those territories, all the moral and material assistance necessary to continue their struggle for the restoration of their inalienable right to self-determination and independence (Ibid).

Resolution 2795—XXVI was approved by a roll-call vote of 105 to 8, with 5 abstentions. The draft text to that effect was based on a proposal in the Fourth Committee by the following 38 Members: Afghanistan, Algeria, Cameroon, Ceylon, Chad, the Congo, Dahomey, Equatorial Guinea, Ethiopia, Ghana, Guinea, India, Indonesia, Iraq, Kenya, Liberia, Malaysia, Mali, Mauritania, Mongolia, Morocco, Niger, Nigeria, Pakistan, Rwanda, Senegal, Sierra Leone, Singapore, Somalia, Sudan, Togo, Tunisia, Uganda, Tanzania, Upper Volta, Yugoslavia, Zaire, and Zambia (UN YB, 1971).

The GA followed up on the recommendation contained in the proposed programme on 20 December 1971, with the adoption of Resolution 2878 (XXVI). This resolution was approved by a recorded vote of 96 to 5, with eighteen abstentions. Resolution 2878—XXVI was based on the proposal of Afghanistan, Algeria, Burundi, Cameroon, the Congo, Egypt, Equatorial Guinea, Ethiopia, Ghana, Guinea, India, Indonesia, Iraq, Kenya, the Libyan Arab Republic, Mali, Mongolia, Morocco, Nigeria, the People's Democratic Republic of Yemen, Rwanda, Sierra Leone, Somalia, Sudan, the Syrian Arab Republic, Tunisia, Uganda, Tanzania, Yemen, Yugoslavia, Zaire, and Zambia (UN YB, 1971).

By Resolution 2878 (XXVI), the GA appealed to all States and the specialised agencies and other organisations within the UN system to provide, in consultation, as appropriate, with the OAU, moral and material assistance to all peoples struggling for their freedom and independence in the colonial territories and, in particular, to the national liberation movements of the territories in Southern Africa, and in that connection drew the attention of all States to the Assistance Fund for the Struggle against Colonialism and Apartheid of the OAU (A/RES 2878—XXVI, 1971).

Also, by the same text, the Assembly endorsed the Special Committee on Independence's proposal to take steps, in consultation with the OAU, to enable representatives of national liberation movements in the colonial Territories in Southern Africa to participate, whenever necessary and in an appropriate capacity, in its deliberations relating to those territories (Ibid).

At the Twenty-Seventh General Assembly, the GA adopted several decisions that acknowledged the increased role of the national liberation movements in the decolonisation process. Thus, the Special Committee on Independence considered inviting, in consultation with and through the OAU, representatives of the liberation movements concerned to participate, whenever necessary and in an 'observer capacity,' in its proceedings relating to their respective countries (UN YB, 1972).

The Special Committee also recommended that the GA make the necessary financial provision to cover the costs of the movement's participation in the Committee's work during 1973. These recommendations were outlined in the form of GA Resolution 2908—XXVII, adopted on 2 November 1972, by a roll-call vote of 99 to 5, with twenty-three abstentions (Ibid).

Resolution 2908—XXVII was proposed by the following members; Afghanistan, Algeria, Burundi, Cameroon, Chad, Chile, the Congo, Cyprus, Dahomey, Democratic Yemen, Egypt, Ethiopia, Ghana, Guinea, Guyana, India, Indonesia, Iraq, the Ivory Coast, Jamaica, Jordan, Kenya, Kuwait, Liberia, Libya, Madagascar, Malaysia, Mali, Mauritania, Mauritius, Mongolia, Morocco, Nepal, Niger, Nigeria, Pakistan, Romania, Rwanda, Senegal, Sierra Leone, Somalia, Sudan, the Syrian Arab Republic, Togo, Trinidad and Tobago, Tunisia, Uganda, the Ukrainian SSR, the United Arab Emirates, the United Republic of Tanzania, Upper Volta, Yemen, Yugoslavia, Zaire, and Zambia (Ibid).

Based on the foregoing, Petuse Norah Appolus (SWAPO); T. George Silundika (ZAPU); S.V. Mtambanengwe (ZANU); Sasa Mbala (FNLA); Mesamesa Tshamba (MPLA); Manuel Jorge Marcelino and dos Santos (FRELIMO) took part as observers in the Special Committee on independence's proceedings during 1973 (GA OR, 1975).

Further, on 2 November 1972, the GA took decisions on the question of dissemination of information on decolonisation—thereby acknowledging the role of the liberation movements in the process. Among other things, the Assembly reaffirmed the vital importance of urgently affecting the widest possible dissemination of information on the evils and dangers of colonialism (A RES 2909—XXVII, 1972).

The GA also affirmed the ongoing liberation struggles by colonial peoples (national liberation movements) in Africa and the international community's efforts to eliminate all remaining forms of colonialism (Ibid).

The GA, further, asked the Secretary-General to: continue to take concrete measures through all the media at his disposal, including publications, radio, and television, to give widespread and continuous publicity to the work of the UN in the field of decolonisation, to the situation in the colonial territories and the continuing struggle for liberation being waged by the colonial peoples; and intensify the activities of information centres, particularly in Western Europe, and establish additional ones where appropriate, especially in Southern Africa (Ibid).

In addition, the assembly asked the Secretary-General to maintain a close working relationship with OAU; enlist help from non-governmental organisations in disseminating relevant information; and continue to publish certain specified publications in other languages besides English and French (Ibid).

The Assembly, therefore, asked the Member States, in particular the administering powers, to co-operate fully with the Secretary-General in disseminating information on decolonisation; and invited all states, the specialised agencies, other UN bodies, and non-governmental organisations to undertake, in cooperation with the Secretary-General, and within their respective spheres of competence, the large-scale dissemination of information referred to above (Ibid).

Once again, the GA asked the Secretary-General, in consultation with the Special Committee on Independence, to collect and prepare continuously, for dissemination by the Office of Public Information, basic material, studies and articles relating to various aspects of decolonisation (Ibid).

Those decisions were taken when the GA adopted Resolution 2909—XXVII, by a vote of 113 to 2, with 12 abstentions. Resolution 2909—XXVIIwas adopted based on the proposal by Afghanistan; Algeria; Burundi; Cameroon; Congo; Cyprus; Dahomey; Egypt; Ethiopia; Ghana; Guinea; Guyana; Indonesia; Iran; Ivory Coast; Jamaica; Jordan; Kenya; Kuwait; Liberia; Madagascar; Malaysia; Maldives; Mali; Mauritania; Mauritius; Morocco; Niger; Nigeria;

Pakistan; Romania; Rwanda; Senegal; Sierra Leone; Singapore; Somalia; Sudan; Syrian Arab Republic; Togo; Tunisia; Uganda; United Republic of Tanzania; Upper Volta; Yemen; Yugoslavia; Zaire; and Zambia (UN YB, 1972).

At the same time, the Assembly also decided to request the Secretary-General, in cooperation with the OAU to organise an International Conference of Experts for the Support of Victims of Colonialism and Apartheid in Southern Africa in Oslo, Norway, in 1973. The decision to request the Secretary-General and OAU to organise the conference, which considered a proposal by OAU to convene an international conference against colonialism and apartheid, was embodied in GA Resolution 2910—XXVII, which was adopted by 118 votes to two, with seven abstentions (Ibid).

Resolution 2910—XXVII had 68 sponsors, namely: Afghanistan; Algeria; Argentina; Austria; Barbados; Bulgaria; Burundi; Cameroon; Chad; Chile; Colombia; Congo; Czechoslovakia; Dahomey; Democratic Yemen; Denmark; Egypt; Ethiopia; Finland; Gabon; Gambia; Ghana; Guinea; Guyana; Iceland; India; Iran; Ireland; Ivory Coast; Jamaica; Jordan; Kenya; Kuwait; Lebanon; Liberia; Libyan Arab Republic; Madagascar; Mali; Mauritania; Mauritius; Mexico; Morocco; Niger; Nigeria; Norway; Pakistan; Peru; Poland; Romania; Rwanda; Senegal, Sierra Leone; Somalia; Sudan; Sweden; Syrian Arab Republic; Togo; Trinidad and Tobago; Tunisia; Turkey; Uganda; United Arab Emirates; United Republic of Tanzania; Upper Volta; Yemen; Yugoslavia; Zaire; and Zambia (Ibid).

In addition, the GA adopted a resolution by which, after noting with satisfaction the progress towards national independence made by the national liberation movements in the colonial territories of Southern Africa and Guinea (Bissau) and Cape Verde, it appealed to the Governments and people of the world to hold annually a Week of Solidarity with the Colonial Peoples of Southern Africa and Guinea (Bissau) and Cape Verde Fighting for Freedom, Independence, and Equal Rights (A/RES 2911—XXVII, 1972).

The Assembly also proposed that a week should begin each year on 25 May, which was Africa Liberation Day. Therefore, it recommended that during the week, meetings be held, and appropriate materials published in the press and broadcast media, and public campaigns conducted to solicit contributions the OAU's Assistance Fund for the Struggle against Colonialism and Apartheid (Ibid).

Those decisions were outlined in resolution 2911—XXVII. The text of this resolution was adopted by 91 votes to 2, with 30 abstentions, on the proposal of Afghanistan; Algeria; Bulgaria; Burundi; Byelorussian SSR; Cameroon; Chile; Congo; Cuba; Czechoslovakia; Dahomey; Egypt; Ghana; Guinea; Hungary; India; Jamaica; Jordan; Kuwait; Liberia; Madagascar; Mauritius; Mongolia; Morocco; Nigeria; Pakistan; Poland; Romania; Rwanda; Senegal; Sierra Leone; Somalia; Sudan; Togo; Tunisia; Uganda; Ukrainian SSR; USSR; United Republic of Tanzania; Upper Volta; Yugoslavia; and Zambia (UN YB, 1972).

On 14 November 1972, the GA adopted a resolution by which, among other things, it expressed its appreciation for the concrete programs of assistance to national liberation movements initiated by several Governments, and also expressed its satisfaction at the progress towards national independence and freedom made by the national liberation movements of the territories—particularly in the liberated areas of Guinea-Bissau by PAIGC, the sole representative of the people of Guinea-Bissau and Cape Verde (A/RES 2980 XXVII, 1972).

The Assembly further affirmed that the national liberation movements of Angola, Guinea-Bissau, Cape Verde, and Mozambique were the authentic representatives of the true aspirations of the peoples of those territories; and, recommended that, pending the territories' accession to independence, all Governments, the specialised agencies and other organisations with the UN system and the UN bodies concerned should when dealing with matters about the territories, ensure their representation by the liberation movements concerned in an appropriate capacity and consultation with the OAU (Ibid).

In addition, the Assembly appealed to all governments, UN bodies, and non-governmental organisations to provide all necessary moral and material assistance to the peoples of the territories, especially those in liberated areas, for their continued struggle for self-determination and independence. Those decisions were outlined in Resolution 2980— XXVII.

Adopted on the recommendation of the Fourth Committee, Resolution 2980—XXVII was adopted by the Assembly, on 14 November 1972, by a roll-call vote of 98 to 6, with 8 abstentions. Resolution 2980 (XXVII) was sponsored by the following powers:

Afghanistan, Bulgaria, the Byelorussian SSR, Cameroon, the Congo, Czechoslovakia, Democratic Yemen, Egypt, Ethiopia, Ghana, Guinea, Guyana, Hungary, India, Indonesia, Iran, Iraq, Kenya, Mali, Mongolia, Nigeria, Romania, Rwanda, Sierra Leone, Somalia, Sudan, the Syrian Arab Republic, Trinidad and Tobago, Tunisia, Uganda, the Ukrainian SSR, Tanzania, Yemen, Yugoslavia, Zaire, and Zambia (UN YB, 1972).

At its 1972 session, the GA also adopted a resolution 2955—XXVII, concerning the importance of the universal realisation of the right of peoples to self-determination and the speedy granting of independence to colonial countries and peoples for the effective guarantee and observance of human rights. Under this resolution, which was adopted on 12 December 1972, the Assembly, among other things, reaffirmed the legitimacy of the peoples' struggle for self-determination and liberation from colonial and alien domination and foreign subjugation by all available means consistent with the UN Charter (A/RES 2955—XXVII, 1972).

The Assembly, also, condemned: all the governments, particularly the governments of Portugal and South Africa, which persistently refused to implement the 1960 Declaration on Independence and other relevant resolutions; the policies of those States members of NATO and other powers that assisted Portugal and other racist regimes in Africa and elsewhere in their suppression of the peoples' human rights; and decided to examine ways and means of extending maximum assistance to the peoples of the liberated areas, colonial territories, and territories under alien subjugation (Ibid).

At the following session, the GA adopted resolutions 3115—XXVIII and 3111—XXVIII, reaffirming decisions already taken by the Special Committee on Independence explicitly recognising the national liberation movements. Adopted on the recommendation of the Fourth Committee, Resolution 3115—XXVIII was approved by the Assembly on 12 December 1973, with a recorded vote of 108 to 4, with fifteen abstentions (UN YB, 1973).

Resolution 3115—XXVIII was put forward in the Fourth Committee by Afghanistan, Bulgaria, Burundi, the Byelorussian SSR, Cameroon, the Central African Republic, Chad, the Congo, Cuba, Czechoslovakia, Dahomey, Democratic Yemen, Egypt, Ethiopia, the Gambia, the German Democratic Republic, Ghana, Guinea, Guyana, Hungary, Iraq, Jordan, Kenya, Kuwait, Liberia, Libya, Madagascar, Mali, Mauritania, Mauritius, Mongolia, Morocco, Nepal, Niger, Nigeria,

Romania, Senegal, Sierra Leone, Somalia, Sudan, Syria, Trinidad and Tobago, Uganda, the Ukrainian SSR, the United Arab Emirates, the United Republic of Tanzania, Upper Volta, Yemen, Yugoslavia, Zaire, and Zambia (Ibid).

Under Resolution 3115—XXVIII, the Assembly, among other things: reaffirmed the principle that there should be no independence before majority rule in Zimbabwe; and stated that any settlement relating to the future of the territory should be worked out with the full participation of the genuine political leaders and representatives of the national liberation movements, who were the sole and authentic representatives of the true aspirations of the people of Zimbabwe, and should be endorsed freely and fully by the people (A/RES 3115—XXVIII, 1973).

Also, adopted on the recommendation of the Fourth Committee, Resolution 3111 (XXVIII) was approved by the GA with a recorded vote of 107 to 2, with 17 abstentions. The resolution was sponsored in the Fourth Committee by the following Members: Afghanistan, Burundi, Cameroon, the Central African Republic, Chad, the Congo, Dahomey, the Gambia, Ghana, Guinea, Guyana, Iraq, Kenya, Liberia, the Libyan Arab Republic, Madagascar, Mali, Mauritania, Morocco, Nepal, Niger, Nigeria, Pakistan, Romania, Senegal, Sierra Leone, Somalia, Sudan, the Syrian Arab Republic, Togo, Uganda, the United Republic of Tanzania, Upper Volta, Yugoslavia, Zaire, and Zambia (UN YB, 1973).

In Resolution 3111 (XXVIII), the GA, among other things: recognised that the national liberation movement of Namibia, the SWAPO, was the authentic representative of the Namibian people; supported the efforts of the movement to strengthen national unity; and appealed for the support of specialised agencies and other organisations within the UN system, in consultation with the UN Council for Namibia, to render, within their respective spheres of competence, all possible assistance to the people of Namibia and their liberation movement (A/RES 3111—XXVIII, 1973).

The implementation by specialised agencies and international institutions associated with the Declaration of Independence, the GA, among other things: noted once again with deep concern that many of the specialised agencies had not extended their full cooperation to the UN in implementing resolutions relating to assistance for the national liberation movements and to ending all kinds of support to Portugal and South Africa, and to the illegal regime in Southern Rhodesia (UN YB, 1973).

The Assembly also urged the specialised agencies and other concerned organisations, in consultation with the OAU, to initiate and broaden contacts and cooperation with the colonial peoples of Africa. This was done to develop concrete assistance programmes for the peoples of Angola, Mozambique, Southern Rhodesia, and Namibia, especially their liberation movements (Ibid).

It further, urged the specialised agencies and other organisations to take measures to withhold any financial, economic, technical, or other assistance from Portugal, South Africa, and the illegal regime in Southern Rhodesia; to discontinue all kinds of support to them until they renounce their policies of racial discrimination and colonial oppression, and to refrain from any action implying recognition of the legitimacy of those regimes' colonial and alien domination of the territories concerned (Ibid).

Those decisions were embodied in GA Resolution 3118—XXVIII of 12 December 1973. Resolution 3118—XXVIII was adopted by a recorded vote of 108 to 4, with 17 abstentions. Resolution 3118 (XXVIII) was proposed in the Fourth Committee by the following countries: Afghanistan, Bulgaria, Burundi, the Byelorussian SSR, Cameroon, the Central African Republic, Chad, the Congo, Czechoslovakia, Dahomey, Democratic Yemen, Egypt, Ethiopia, the Gambia, the German Democratic Republic, Ghana, Guinea, Hungary, India, Indonesia, Iran, Iraq, Kenya, Liberia, Madagascar, Mali, Mauritania, Mongolia, Morocco, Niger, Nigeria, Romania, Rwanda, Senegal, Sierra Leone, Somalia, Sudan, the Syrian Arab Republic, Togo, Tunisia, Uganda, the Ukrainian SSR, the United Republic of Tanzania, Upper Volta, Yugoslavia, Zaire, and Zambia (Ibid).

The international recognition of the national liberation movements was reaffirmed in 1973 when the GA adopted Resolution 3163—XXVIII, by a recorded vote of 104 to 5, with 19 abstentions. Resolution 3163 (XXVIII) was adopted on the proposal of the 59 member states (UN YB, 1973).

Under Resolution 3163 (XXVIII), the Assembly, among other things, appealed to all states, the specialised agencies, and other organisations within the UN system to provide moral and material assistance to all peoples struggling for their freedom and independence in the colonial territories and to those living under alien domination—

in particular to the national liberation movements of the territories in Africa—in consultation, as appropriate, with the OAU (A/RES 3163—XXVIII, 1973).

The GA, further appealed to all governments and the specialized agencies and other organisations within the UN system, in consultation with the OAU, to ensure the representation of the colonial territories in Africa by the national liberation movements concerned, in an appropriate capacity, when dealing with matters about those territories (Ibid).

The adoption of Resolution 3163—XXVIII was based on the Assembly decision of 2 November 1972. By this decision, the GA had approved the Special Committee on independence's arrangement in consultation with the OAU, to invite representatives of the national liberation movements of the colonial territories in Africa to participate as observers in its proceedings relating to the movements' respective countries (already discussed above).

In adopting Resolution 3163—XXVIII, the Assembly also considered the views expressed by the national liberation movements and non-governmental organisations which participated, along with several members of the Special Committee on Independence, in the proceedings of the International Conference of Experts for the Support of Victims of Colonialism and Apartheid in Southern Africa, held from 9 to 14 April 1973, at Oslo, Norway (Sechaba, 1973).

Some of the views were expressed by Oliver Tambo, President of the ANC, on behalf of all national liberation movements. Tambo stated that the keyword in the declared purpose of the Conference was 'support,' which should have been interpreted as the practical measure and material assistance that the world community was prepared to give to the liberation movements in their growing offensives against the racist regimes in Southern Africa (Sechaba, 1973).

In 1973 and 1974, the GA and on occasions the ECOSOC also adopted recommendations and decisions on an Ad Hoc basis concerning the participation of national liberation movements in international conferences. Thus, at its twenty-eighth session, the Assembly followed up with Resolution 3102—XXVIII, on 12 December 1973 (UN YB, 1973).

Resolution 3102 (XXVIII) was adopted by a recorded vote of 107 to 0, with six abstentions on the recommendation of the Sixth (Legal) Committee. In the preamble of the resolution, the GA reaffirmed that complete respect for the UN Charter and general and complete disarmament under effective international control were essential to prevent armed conflicts and their suffering. It expressed its determination to continue efforts towards this goal (A/RES 3102—XXVIII, 1973).

The Assembly also noted that armed conflicts continued to cause untold human suffering and material devastation and expressed its conviction that in all such conflicts, rules were needed to reduce the suffering and increase the protection of non-combatants and civilian objects (Ibid).

Further, the GA reaffirmed the urgent need to ensure full and effective application by all parties to armed conflicts of existing legal rules relating to such conflicts, in particular, The Hague Conventions of 1899 and 1907, the Geneva Protocol of 1925 and the Geneva Conventions of 1949, and to consider modern developments in methods and means of warfare (Ibid).

Under the operative part of the resolution, the Assembly, among other things, expressed its appreciation to the Swiss Federal Council for convoking in 1974, the Diplomatic Conference on the Reaffirmation and Development of International Humanitarian Law Applicable in Armed Conflicts (IHL); and urged that the national liberation movements recognised by the various regional inter-governmental organisations concerned be invited to participate in the Conference as observers, according to the practice of the UN (Ibid).

The Assembly furthermore urged participants in the Conference to do their utmost to reach an agreement on additional rules which might help to alleviate the suffering brought by armed conflicts and to protect non-combatants and civilian objects in such conflicts; and appealed to all parties to armed conflicts to acknowledge, and comply with, their obligations under humanitarian instruments and to observe the applicable international humanitarian rules (Ibid).

In the following session, the GA adopted two key resolutions. On 29 November 1974, the Assembly decided to invite all States to participate in the UN Conference on the Representation of States in Their Relations with International Organisations (See Chapter Five). It was also decided to invite the national liberation movements recognised by the OAU and/or the League of Arab States (LAS) in their respective regions, to participate as observers in that Conference, following UN practice (UN YB, 1974).

Those decisions were embodied in Resolution 3247—XXVIII, which was adopted by 105 votes to 3, with 15 abstentions. The resolution was based on the proposal of: Algeria; Botswana; Egypt; Ghana; Guyana; the Ivory Coast; Kenya; Lesotho; the Libyan Arab Republic; Mali; Nigeria; Somalia; the Syrian Arab Republic; Tunisia; the United Republic of Tanzania; and Yugoslavia (Ibid).

On 10 December 1974, the Assembly, under its decision of 18 December 1972, decided to invite all States to participate in the Conference of the International Women's Year (See chapter five for details concerning this Conference), and to invite the national liberation movements recognised by the OAU and/or by the LAS to participate as observers, regularly and in accordance with earlier practice of the UN. This decision was embodied in Resolution 3276—XXVIII. The resolution was approved, by 124 votes to two, with two abstentions. Resolution 3276—XXVIII was based on a proposal by Australia, Belgium, Iran, Nepal, Norway, the Philippines, Sierra Leone, Senegal, and Sweden (UN YB, 1974).

Towards the end of the twenty-ninth session, the GA took a more comprehensive decision relating to the growing recognition of the national liberation movements. This was in the form of Resolution 3280—XXIX of December 1974. With Resolution 3280—XXIX, the Assembly decided to invite as observers, on a regular basis and by earlier practice, representatives of the national liberation movements recognised by the OAU to participate in the relevant work of the Main Committees of the GA and its subsidiary organs concerned (A/RES 3280 XXIX, 1974).

The GA also invited those representatives to participate in the same capacity in conferences, seminars, and other meetings held under the auspices of the UN related to their countries, and requested the Secretary-General, in consultation with the OAU, to ensure that the necessary arrangements were made for their effective participation, including the requisite financial provisions (Ibid).

The GA, further, recommended to the other UN organs concerned, in consultation with the OAU, to ensure that the necessary arrangements are made to facilitate the effective participation of these national liberation movements in their relevant proceedings; and requested the Secretary-General to submit to the GA at its thirtieth session a report on the implementation of the resolution and the development of co-operation between the OAU and the organisations concerned within the UN (Ibid).

Resolution 3280—XXIX was sponsored in the GA by 42 member States of the OAU, namely: Algeria; Botswana; Burundi; Central African Republic; Chad; Congo; Dahomey; Egypt; Equatorial Guinea; Ethiopia, Gabon; Gambia; Ghana; Guinea; Guinea-Bissau; Ivory Coast; Kenya; Lesotho; Liberia; Libyan Arab Republic; Madagascar; Malawi; Mali; Mauritania; Mauritius; Morocco; Niger; Nigeria; Rwanda; Senegal; Sierra Leone; Somalia; Sudan; Swaziland; Togo; Tunisia; Uganda; United Republic of Cameroon; United Republic of Tanzania; Upper Volta; Zaire; and Zambia (UN YB, 1974).

At its 2318th meeting, on 13 December 1974, the Assembly adopted Resolution 3300 (XXIX), on the implementation of the Declaration on Independence by the specialised agencies and the international institutions associated with the UN. Adopted without objection on the recommendation of the Fourth Committee, this resolution set forth the GA's decisions on the question (Ibid).

The sponsors of the resolution were: Afghanistan, Bulgaria, Burundi, the Byelorussian SSR, the Central African Republic, the Congo, Cuba, Czechoslovakia, Democratic Yemen, Egypt, Ethiopia, Gabon, the German Democratic Republic, Ghana, Hungary, India, Indonesia, Iran, Iraq, the Ivory Coast, Kenya, Liberia, Mongolia, Nigeria, Pakistan, Poland, Romania, Rwanda, Sierra Leone, the Syrian Arab Republic, Togo, Trinidad and Tobago, Tunisia, Uganda, the Ukrainian SSR, the United Arab Emirates, the United Republic of Tanzania, Upper Volta, Yugoslavia, Zaire, and Zambia (Ibid).

By the preamble of the resolution, the Assembly, among other things, expressed its awareness of the urgent and pressing need of the peoples in colonial territories in Africa for concrete assistance from the specialised agencies and other institutions associated with the UN in the administration of their countries and the reconstruction programmes being undertaken by their national liberation movements (A/RES 3300—XXIX, 1974).

The GA also noted with satisfaction the measures taken by several agencies and organisations within the UN system to grant observer status to the national liberation movements; and expressed the hope that other organisations would take the necessary steps in that regard (Ibid).

It further welcomed the categorical renunciation by the Government of Portugal of the colonialist policy of its predecessors, in particular the unequivocal acceptance by that Government of its obligations under the relevant provisions of the Charter and its recognition of the right of the peoples concerned to self-determination and independence (Ibid).

Under the resolution's operative provisions, the GA approved the Special Committee's report chapter on independence and reaffirmed that the recognition of colonial peoples' legitimate struggle for freedom by the Assembly, SC, and other UN bodies necessitated the full extension of moral and material assistance from the UN system to these peoples, including those in liberated areas of the colonial territories and their national liberation movements (Ibid).

The Assembly also urged all the specialised agencies and institutions associated with the United Nations and all States to give, as a matter of urgency, all possible moral and material assistance to the peoples in Africa struggling for their liberation from colonial rule and, in particular, recommended that the organisations concerned initiate or broaden contacts and co-operation with those peoples in consultation with OAU and work out and implement concrete programs for such assistance, with the active collaboration of the national liberation movements concerned (Ibid).

The GA, again asked the specialised agencies and other organisations, particularly the United Nations Development Programme (UNDP) and the World Bank, to increase the scope and flexibility of their assistance to refugees; and urged once again that those agencies and organisations take all necessary measures to withhold any financial, economic, technical or other assistance from the Government of South Africa and the illegal regime in Southern Rhodesia, discontinue all support to them until they restored to the peoples of Namibia and Zimbabwe their inalienable right to self-determination and independence, and refrain from taking any action which might imply recognition of the legitimacy of the domination of the territories by those regimes (Ibid).

It, further, requested the specialised agencies and other organisations within the UN system to make appropriate procedural arrangements to enable representatives of the national liberation movements of the colonial territories recognised by OAU to participate fully as observers in all proceedings relating to their countries, particularly to ensure that assistance projects of the agencies and organisations were carried out to the benefit of the national liberation movements and peoples of the liberated areas (Ibid).

The Assembly, therefore, recommended that all governments intensify efforts within UN specialised agencies and organizations to ensure full implementation of the Declaration on Independence and other relevant UN resolutions. Accordingly, that action would ensure the full and effective implementation of the Declaration on Independence and other relevant UN resolutions; and would also provide emergency assistance to the colonial territories and their national liberation movements on a priority basis (Ibid).

To facilitate such action, the GA urged the executive heads of the specialised agencies and other organisations within the UN system to formulate and submit to their respective governing bodies or legislative organs, as a matter of priority and with the active cooperation of OAU, concrete proposals for the full implementation of the relevant UN decisions, particularly, specific programmes of all possible assistance to the peoples in colonial territories and their national liberation movements, together with a comprehensive analysis of the problems, if any, confronted by those agencies and organisations (Ibid).

The increased acknowledgment of the role of the national liberation movements in the decolonisation process was further revealed by additional international instruments and norms for the protection of freedom fighters. The GA frequently appealed for the application of the 1949 Geneva and 1907 Hague Conventions' provisions to members of liberation movements' armed forces (UN YB, 1974).

Resolution 2621—XXV contained such appeals and reiterated some of the principles already outlined in previous Assembly resolutions and, particularly, laid down that 'armed conflicts involving the struggle of peoples against colonial and alien domination and racist regimes were to be regarded as international armed conflicts in the sense of the 1949 Geneva Conventions' (Ibid).

In Resolution 2674—XXV of 9 December 1970, the GA, among other things, condemned the actions of countries that, in flagrant violation of the Charter, continued to conduct aggressive wars and defy accepted principles of the Geneva Protocol of 1925 and the Geneva Conventions of 1949 (A/RES 2674—XXV, 1970).

The Assembly also affirmed that the participants in resistance movements and the freedom fighters in Southern Africa and territories under colonial and alien domination and foreign occupation—struggling for their liberation and self-determination—should be treated, in case of their arrest, as prisoners of war by the Hague Convention of 1907 and the Geneva Conventions of 1949 (Ibid).

By the operative part of Resolution 2852—XXVI of 20 December 1971, the GA, among other things, called again upon all parties to any armed conflict to observe the rules laid down in The Hague Conventions of 1899 and 1907, the Geneva Protocol of 1925, the Geneva Conventions of 1949 and other humanitarian rules applicable in armed conflicts and invited those States which had not yet done so to adhere to those instruments (A/RES 2852—XXVI, 1971).

The Assembly, further, reaffirmed that persons participating in resistance movements and freedom fighters in Southern Africa and territories under colonial and alien domination and foreign occupation who were struggling for their liberation and self-determination should, in case of arrest, be treated as prisoners of war by the principles of The Hague Convention of 1907 and the Geneva Conventions of 1949 (Ibid).

At its twenty-eighth session, on 12 December 1973, the GA adopted Resolution 3103—

XXVII. Its adoption implied that force used by national liberation movements or third States to resist denial of self-determination was, in fact, legitimate under the UN Charter (Higgins, 2004) Resolution 3103—XXVII was a relatively short but revolutionary resolution that placed the national liberation, particularly their struggle, within the ambit of international law and following the UN and the Universal Declaration of Human Rights (Houser, 1973).

Under Resolution 3103—XXVII, the Assembly proclaimed six basic principles of the legal status of combatants struggling against colonial and alien domination and racist regimes. The first of the six principles was that the struggle of peoples under colonial and alien domination and racist regimes for the implementation of their right to self-determination and independence was legitimate and in full accordance with the principles of international law (A/RES 3103—XXVII, 1973).

Second, any attempt to suppress the struggle against colonial and alien domination and racist regimes was deemed incompatible with the

UN Charter, the Declaration on Principles of International Law, the Universal Declaration of Human Rights, and the Declaration on Independence, thus constituting a threat to international peace and security (Ibid).

Third was that the armed conflicts involving the struggle of peoples against colonial and alien domination and racist regimes were to be regarded as international armed conflicts in the sense of the 1949 Geneva Conventions, and the legal status envisaged to apply to the combatants in those Conventions and other international instruments was to apply to the persons engaged in armed struggle against colonial and alien domination and racist regimes (Ibid).

Fourth was that the combatants struggling against colonial and alien domination and racist regimes captured as prisoners were to be accorded the status of prisoners of war and their treatment should be by the provisions of the Geneva Convention relative to the Treatment of Prisoners of War, of 12 August 1949 (Ibid).

The fifth principle was that the use of mercenaries by colonial and racist regimes against the national liberation movements struggling for their freedom and independence from the yoke of colonialism and alien domination was a criminal act and the mercenaries should accordingly be punished as criminals (Ibid).

The last principle was that the violation of the legal status of the combatants struggling against colonial and alien domination and racist regimes during armed conflicts entailed full responsibility by the norms of international law (Ibid).

Collectively, these principles established norms for the use of armed force in non-international conflicts domestically, while also signifying UN support of the legality of the national liberation movements' struggle against colonialism, alien domination, and racism (Ibid).

## 3.3 Conclusion

This chapter discusses reactions and responses to the representation of national liberation movements at the UN. The UN's acknowledgment of liberation movements' role in decolonisation was a major reaction to their representation. As discussed, their acknowledgement was expressed by offering aid to them, via the OAU; and, by inviting their representatives to participate in the proceedings and deliberations of the Main Committees of the UN GA and its organs and agencies, observers. In a sense, and as illustrated, the UN came to play closer to the national liberation movements than the colonial powers, by adopting decisions that pushed the movements higher on the political ladder. This initiative began with UN appeals to member states for the moral and material support to the liberation movements. The UN later decided to treat members of African liberation movements in accordance with international armed conflict and human rights laws, effectively incorporating them into the UN system legally. Voting on GA decisions, particularly from 1965-1974, clearly indicated a significant recognition of liberation movements' role within the UN system. The unanimous adoption of these decisions was another major reaction and response to the representation of the national liberation movements in the UN. The next chapter discusses the OAU's role in the representation of national liberation movements at the UN.

# CHAPTER FOUR

## The Role of OAU on Representation of National Liberation Movements at the UN, 1963-1974

### 4.1 Introduction

This chapter's first section introduces the OAU's role in the representation of national liberation movements at the UN. The next section describes the OAU decisions on supporting and aiding the national liberation movements, especially those adopted between 1963 and 1974, to outline the organisation's role in their UN representation. The third section concludes the chapter.

Upon its foundation in 1963, the OAU asserted its primary goal of spearheading the decolonisation process. That included the struggle against colonialism, apartheid, and the decolonisation of the remaining colonial territories in Africa (Boavida et al., 2010). It named colonialism and apartheid as threats to African peace and security; violated the inalienable rights; and opposed the principles of self-determination and independence. Initially, the OAU stressed that those political ills should be eradicated peacefully without bloodshed. However, in Namibia, Zimbabwe, and Portuguese territories, the use of force became inevitable due to circumstances (OAU, 1963).

Consequently, the OAU decided to militarily aid and support national liberation movements in those territories. The aid and support provided by the OAU included various forms, such as diplomatic action on their behalf. One weapon for this diplomacy was the recognition by the OAU of the national liberation movements as authentic representatives of colonial countries and peoples. The criteria for recognising the movements were based on their 'representativeness' and effectiveness in their struggles (Faundez, 1989). The Liberation Committee was the OAU organ responsible for recognising the movements (Yousuf, 1985). Recognition by OAU of the liberation movements was significant for their legal standing in the UN (Mastorodimos, 2025) because it conditioned and determined the world body's actions concerning colonialism and apartheid (Boavida, et.al, 2010).

Arguably, the OAU played a colossal role in the representation of the national liberation movements at the UN. The representation of liberation movements at the UN is a significant pointer because it gave legitimacy to the liberation struggle against racism and colonialism in Africa. It is also significant because it provided independent African states with machinery to supply the liberation movements with material and other aid needed to wage their armed struggles. In particular, it is critical because it set in motion a unified African policy toward colonial and settler regimes in Africa; and enabled the regional body to solicit international support for the liberation efforts in Southern Africa (El-Khawas, 1978). It is, further, a significant pointer because it reflected developments in the new international legal order of the last half of the twentieth century in which the right to self-determination had become entrenched in the *Jus cogens*, basic, fundamental, imperative, or overriding rules of international law, peremptory norms which could not be set aside by treaty or acquiescence but only by the formation of a subsequent norm of contrary effect (Barat, 1990). Further, it is a significant pointer because it legitimised the move by the GA (Shaw, 1983) to secure greater information regarding developments in particular territories, thereby implicitly acknowledging a kind of superior status in respect of the national liberation movements in African territories. This legitimisation was in the form of granting the movements recognised by the OAU an 'observer' status in the UN GA main committees and organs (Mastorodimos, 2015). The OAU's initiative to link liberation movements with the UN was a strategically executed diplomatic move. This action represented the first formal institutional connection that initiated discussions between the OAU and the UN specifically concerning decolonisation (Gorelick, 1986). This linkage creates a gap that is yet to be scholarly addressed in Africa's diplomatic history.

To understand the OAU's role in the representation of national liberation movements at the UN, one must begin by examining the continental body's decisions regarding their recognition. This requires examining those that were adopted during the period between 1963 and 1974. Although not legally binding on the OAU member states (Paterson, 2013), an analysis of the OAU decisions on recognition of the movements is critical because they suggested diplomatic action against colonial powers in Africa, such as South Africa, Southern Rhodesia, and Portugal, as well as appropriate action in the UN and severance of diplomatic relations (Binaisa, 1977).

The non-binding nature of these resolutions impacted the OAU's support for national liberation movements as they failed to deter states like Malawi from maintaining diplomatic ties with white white minority regimes, especially South Africa. In 1971, for example, President Kamuzu Banda made a state visit to South Africa to the chagrin of other African leaders (Miller, 2015).

An examination of the OAU decisions on recognition of the movements is also critical because they moulded the international public opinion and influenced it by the active pursuit of the OAU goals through aggressive participation in international fora on behalf of the liberation movements in their struggle against colonialism and apartheid (Tekkle, 1988). For example, the OAU, through the UN forced South Africa out of the ECA, the Food and Agriculture Organisation (FAO), the International Labour Organisation (ILO), and even the Olympic games (Binaisa, 1977).

Also, the OAU generated pressure on other countries to sever relations with Southern Rhodesia (Ibid). Similarly, the OAU through the UN internationalised the Portuguese colonial policy by addressing the situation within territories. This involved adopting decisions and promoting initiatives to persuade Portugal towards decolonisation (Santos, 2012).

## 4.2 The OAU Executive Council Decisions on the Support and Assistance for the National Liberation Movements, 1963-1974

During the period between 1963 and 1974, the OAU adopted several resolutions and recommendations that revealed its commitment to support the national liberation movements struggling against colonialism and apartheid in Southern Africa. In a general sense, African states such as Tanzania, Zambia and Congo (Brazzaville), responded to these resolutions and recommendations by allowing the national liberation movements to establish their offices and centres there (Houser, 1967). Significantly, these centres were crucial for members of national liberation movements to intermingle, created synergies, exchanged ideas, and share knowledge (Grilli, 2021). As an indication of the general, actions and decisions of the independent

African states concerning their support for national liberation were welcomed by representatives of the movements

The first of these resolutions was adopted at the First Summit Conference of the Assembly of Heads of State and Government in May 1963. This resolution was under Agenda Item II entitled 'Decolonisation (OAU, 1963). Under the resolution, the Assembly reaffirmed its support of African nationalists in Zimbabwe and solemnly declared if the territory were to be usurped by a racial white minority government, State Members of OAU would lend their effective moral and practical support to any legitimate measures that the African nationalist might have devised to recover such power and restore it to the African majority; and the Conference undertaking henceforth to concert the efforts of its Members to take such measures as the situation demanded against any State according to recognition to the minority (OAU, 1963).

The Assembly, also, reaffirmed further, that the territory of Namibia was an African territory under the international mandate and that any attempt by the Republic of South Africa to annex it would be regarded as an act of aggression; and reaffirmed also its determination to render all necessary support to the second phase of Namibia before the International Court of Justice (ICJ); and reaffirmed, still further the inalienable right of the people of that territory to self-determination and independence (Ibid).

In addition, the Assembly, pleaded with the Great Powers (such as Portugal, Spain, the Dutch Republic, France, and England) so that they cease, without exception, to lend their direct or indirect support or assistance to all those colonial governments which might use such assistance to suppress national liberation movements, particularly the Portuguese Government which was conducting a real war of genocide in Africa (Ibid).

The Assembly, therefore, earnestly, invited all national liberation movements to coordinate their efforts establishing common action fronts wherever necessary to strengthen the effectiveness of their struggle and the rational use of the concerted assistance given to them— strengthen the effectiveness of their struggle and the rational use of the concerted assistance given to them (Ibid).

During its Second Ordinary Session, held in Lagos, Nigeria, from 24 to 29 February 1964, the Council of Ministers adopted resolutions on apartheid in South Africa; and Zimbabwe. By the resolution on apartheid in South Africa, the Council, requested that the delegation approach the UN SC so that the latter should take all necessary steps as soon as possible to implement its resolutions S/5386 (7 August 1963) and S/5471 (4 December 1963), concerning the discontinuation of the mockeries of trials (main one being the 1963- 1964 Treason Trial) given to South African nationalists and the release of all those persons who were imprisoned, interned or subjected to other restrictions for having opposed apartheid (CM/RES 13—II, 1964).

With the resolution on Zimbabwe, the Council called on the Liberation Committee of the OAU to strengthen its support to the courageous African nationalists so that they might intensify the struggle and carry it to its logical conclusion with independence based on the principle of 'one man, one choice (CM/RES 14—II, 1964).

At the next Session, in July 1964, the Council of Ministers adopted further resolutions for Zimbabwe; the Portuguese Administered Territories and South Africa. The adoption of these resolutions was due to the deteriorating situation there and, brutality resulting from the action of racist regimes in those territories. About Zimbabwe, the Council adopted recommendations for action by the Assembly and the UK Government. In particular, it recommended to the Assembly that it urged the African States to take a vigorous stand against a Declaration of Independence of Zimbabwe (UDI) by a European, minority government; and that those States pledge themselves to take appropriate measures, including recognition and support of an African nationalist government in exile should such an eventuality arise (CM/RES 33—III, 1964).

As for the UK Government, the Council recommended that it be called upon to convene immediately a constitutional conference in which representatives of all political groups in the territory would participate to prepare a revised democratic constitution ensuring majority rule based on 'one man, one vote; and recommended that the UK immediately release Joshua Nkomo (ZAPU), the Reverend Ndabininge Sithole and all other political prisoners and detainees (Ibid).

The Council, further, recommended but without mentioning names, that some Governments offer their good offices to the nationalist parties in Zimbabwe to bring about a united front of all the liberation movements for the rapid attainment of their common objective of independence (Ibid).

It, therefore, appealed to the African Nationalist movements in Zimbabwe to intensify their struggle for immediate independence. Discernibly, the Council' recommendations aimed to unite all stakeholders in Zimbabwe to find common ground for resolving the crisis, specifically to achieve a speedy transition to independence based on majority rule (Ibid).

In response, the Assembly requested the Government of the UK to at once release all political prisoners and detainees; and asked the Governments of Malawi, Tanzania, and Zanzibar to offer their good offices to the nationalist parties in Southern Rhodesia. This was done unite liberation movements for the rapid attainment of independence and to aid their intensified struggle for immediate independence (Ibid).

In a further action, the Assembly appealed to the African States to take a vigorous stand against the UDI by a European minority government. It also requested those States to pledge themselves to take appropriate measures including the recognition and support of an African nationalist government in exile should such an eventuality arise; and the Government of the UK to convene immediately a constitutional conference in which representatives of all political groups in the territory would participate to prepare a revised democratic constitution ensuring majority rule based on 'one man, one vote (Ibid).

As for the Portuguese Administered Territories, the Council recommended that the Assembly condemn Portugal for its persistent refusal to recognise the right of the peoples under its domination to self-determination and independence and for its non-compliance with the resolution of the GA and SC of the UN. It also recommended that the Assembly urge African nationalist movements in Portuguese territories to intensify their struggle for immediate liberation (CM/RES 34—III, 1964).

The Assembly responded by condemning Portugal for refusing to recognise the right of the peoples under its domination to self-determination and independence and for its non-compliance with the resolutions of the UN GA and SC and appealed to the African nationalist movements in the territories under Portuguese administration to intensify their struggle for their immediate liberation (AHG/Res.9—I, 1964).

By the resolution on South Africa, the Council decided, among other things, to submit to the First Assembly of Heads of State and

Government, the following recommendation: to call for the release of Nelson Mandela, Walter Sisulu (leaders of the ANC, South Africa), Mangaliso Sobukwe (leader of the PAC) and all other nationalists imprisoned or detained under the arbitrary laws of South Africa (CM/RES 31—III, 1964).

The Assembly of Heads of State and Government responded by expressing its deep distress at the convictions of and sentences passed on African nationalists, particularly on Mandela and Sisulu Sobukwe and all other nationalists, imprisoned or detained under the arbitrary laws of South Africa (AHG/RES.7—I, 1964).

In October 1965, the Council based on its previous resolutions and those of the Assembly took further actions relating to Zimbabwe, South Africa and the Portuguese Administered territories. Regarding Zimbabwe, the Council, among other things, urged the UK Government to immediately release all the leaders of the nationalist movements, Joshua Nkomo, Ndabaningi Sithole and other political prisoners. It also decided to recommend the Assembly of Heads of State and Government, to give immediate assistance to the people of Zimbabwe to bring about majority rule in the country; and to appoint a special committee to work out all forms of assistance to Southern Rhodesia (CM/RES 62—V, 1965).

The one on South Africa, the Council invited the liberation of the South African people to concert their policies and actions and intensify the struggle for full equality and appealed to all States to lend moral and material assistance to the liberation movements in their struggle (CM/Res66—V, 1965).

Regarding Portuguese colonies, the Council requested neighbouring countries to encourage freedom fighters (liberation movements) to provide war material to aid their liberation struggle. It also requested the liberation movements intensify their internal struggles and unite their efforts against colonialism (CM/Res.67—V, 1965).

The Council, therefore, urged all countries that love the freedom to grant liberation movements in those colonies, aided by the OAU the necessary political and military assistance. Accordingly, this would further lead to a swift and unconditional liberation of respective territories in which the struggle was being waged (CM/RES 67—V, 1965).

Since it was necessary to intensify the armed struggle within the Portuguese-administered territories, the Assembly of Heads of State and Government requested: that the countries surrounding the Portuguese colonies grant the broadest possible freedom of movement of people and materials, necessary for the rapid success of the armed struggle carried out by the liberation movements; and all movements to intensify their struggles within their respective territories, and to come together in concerted action (AHG/Res 35—II, 1965).

The Assembly also invited the Liberation Committee to assist the nationalist movements fighting for liberation within the Portuguese colonies. It also appealed to all freedom-loving countries to grant the liberation movements in Portuguese colonies aided by the OAU all necessary political, diplomatic and military aid with a view to the rapid and unconditional liberation of their respective territories (Ibid). By inviting the Committee, the OAU had come to realise that movements were indeed determined to overthrow the colonial and racist Portuguese administration in those colonies and that it was time for all African countries to lend their support for those movements.

Regarding Zimbabwe, the Council urged the UK Government to release all nationalist movement leaders, including Joshua Nkomo and Rev Ndabaningi Sithole and all other political prisoners (CM/RES 62—V, 1965). However, that did not happen as the UK Government persistently refused to heed the call to grant independence to the territory, based on a majority government.

The Council, also, urged the Government of the UK to hold a constitutional conference with the participation of the duly elected representatives of the entire population of Zimbabwe, to adopt a democratic constitution guaranteeing universal suffrage (one man, one vote) free elections, and independence, as well as to recommend to the Assembly to provide immediate assistance to the people of Zimbabwe (Ibid). However, this call went unheeded, as suffering persisted in Zimbabwe, a fact acknowledged by the Government of the UK.

In response and concerned with the gravity of the situation in Zimbabwe, the Assembly deplored the refusal of the UK Government to state categorically that it would not grant independence to that territory except based on the majority government (AHG/Res.25—II,1965). The Council appealed to the UN to deem the Unilateral Declaration of Independence (UDI) a threat to international peace. It urged the UN to take necessary action under its Charter and assist in establishing a majority government in Zimbabwe (Ibid).

By the same resolution, the Council, further, requested the UK Government, among other things: to release the leader of the nationalist movements, Joshua Nkomo, the Reverend Nbabaningi Sithole and other political prisoners; and to give immediate assistance to the people of Zimbabwe to establisha majority government in the country (Ibid).

The Council took further actions on the situation in Southern Africa, at its Seventh Ordinary Session, in November 1966. Their adoption was, accordingly, based on the Liberation Committee's ability to keep the torch of struggle against colonialism, imperialism and racial discrimination. For Zimbabwe, the Council recommended that the OAU and all friendly governments provide material and financial aid to the people fighting within the territory. It, therefore, appealed to all member countries to contribute to the Special Southern Rhodesian Liberation Fund to enable all Zimbabwe nationalists to intensify fighting against the rebels (CM/RES. 77/REV.1—VII, 1966).

To implement the resolution establishing a Solidarity Committee for Zambia, Member States were urged to provide technical and economic assistance to Zambia. The idea was to enable Zambia to withstand the effects of the UDI and to help the Zimbabwean freedom fighters more effectively (Chongo, 2016).

In addition, and as a way of showing sympathy with the people of Zimbabwe, the Council paid tribute to the freedom fighters who had died in the fight against the racist regime of Southern Rhodesia's usurper forces (CM/RES. 77/REV.1—VII, 1966).

In another resolution on Zimbabwe (CM/Res. 78 (VII) of November 1966), Council, further, appealed to all States to implement the provisions of Resolution 218 (1966) of 23 November 1965, of the UN Security Council, which, reaffirmed the immediate recognition of the right of the people of those territories to self-determination and independence; as well as the promulgation of an unconditional political amnesty and the establishment of conditions that will allow the free functioning of political parties (CM/RES 78—VII, 1966).

The Council, further proposed negotiations, based on the recognition of the right to self-determination, with the authorised representatives of the political parties within and outside the Territories with a view to the transfer of power to political institutions freely elected and representative of the peoples, in accordance with the 1960 Declaration and the granting of independence immediately thereafter to all the territories under its administration following people's aspirations (Ibid).

In addition, the Council appealed to all States to implement the provisions of Resolution 2107 (XX) of 21 December 1965 by the UN GA urging them, among other things, in coordination with the OAU, to render the peoples of the territories under Portuguese administration the moral and material support necessary for the restoration of their inalienable rights (Ibid).

With the resolution on South Africa, the Council, among other things: greeted all those who were struggling against apartheid, particularly in South Africa; and reaffirmed support for humanitarian programmes designed to assist victims of apartheid, including the UN Trust Fund for South Africa, and programmes to grant scholarships, educational facilities and employment opportunities to refugees from South Africa (CM/RE 86—VII, 1966).

The Council, therefore, expressed its support for the decision of the UN GA to proclaim the anniversary of the Sharpeville Massacre, 21 March 1960, as 'International Day for the Elimination of Racial Discrimination'; and urged all African States and Organisations to cooperate in observing the day (Ibid).

Concerning Namibia the Council, among other things: appealed to all Member States to spare no efforts in helping Namibia to rid itself of foreign occupation in order to exercise the inalienable right to freedom and independence; and urged the Liberation Committee to give priority to the termination of the occupation of Namibia [by South Africa] (CM/RES 87—VII, 1966).

Therefore, the Council welcomed the resolution's unequivocal termination of South Africa's mandate over Namibia, asserting South Africa's complete lack of authority in the territory (Ibid).

To that end, the Council appealed to all Member States to help the people of Namibia the people of Namibia achieve freedom and independence from foreign occupation. It also urged the Liberation Committee to give priority to the termination of the occupation of Namibia (Ibid).

At its eighth ordinary session in March 1967, the Council adopted several resolutions concerning Zimbabwe and Namibia. By the resolution on Zimbabwe the Council, condemned the United States for constitutional responsibilities to the people of Zimbabwe by allowing the 'illegal racist regime' of Ian Smith to consolidate its position in defiance of the rights of the people of Zimbabwe and world opinion (CM/RES96—VIII, 1967).

The Council, further, strongly reaffirmed the right of the people of Zimbabwe to freedom and self-determination; and appealed to the nationalist movements in that territory to unite their ranks, coordinate and intensify their efforts against the common enemy to expedite efforts against the common enemy to expedite the liberation of their territory and also to African States to give every assistance to the nationalist movements to ensure the liberation of the territory and the establishment of majority rule (Ibid).

The resolution Namibia Council, referencing the 1960 Declaration on Independence and GA Resolution 2145 (XXI) of 27 October 1966, encouraged the UN Ad Hoc Committee for South West Africa's efforts to enable Namibians to exercise self-determination and achieve independence. It also pledged its support to the Ad Hoc Committee and requested the UN to take all necessary measures for South-West Africa's self-determination and independence (CM/RES 97—VIII, 1967).

The Council followed up with further resolutions at its next session, in September 1967. By a resolution on the Portuguese Administered Territories the Council, earnestly entreated all the nationalist movements to close their ranks, co-ordinate their activities and intensify their struggle to achieve self-determination and independence; and welcomed the resolution adopted and the measures taken by the UN to enable the largest possible number of Africans living under Portuguese domination to benefit from the special training programmes provided by UN specialised agencies (CM/Res.101—IX, 1967).

The Council also urged independent African countries to assist refugees and the liberation movements in Portuguese territories. It also recommended forming a committee (Congo Brazzaville, Congo-Kinshasa, Ghana, Egypt, and Zambia) to study the Angolan situation and encourage Angolan liberation movements to unite for a more effective struggle (Ibid).

By another resolution, the Council paid tribute to all who were struggling tirelessly and effectively against apartheid, especially in South Africa; renewed its support for the humanitarian programmes designed to aid the victims of apartheid, particularly, the UN Trust Fund for South Africa, and the programme providing fellowships and other opportunities of education and employment, for South African refugees; and, appealed to all states to make the twenty-first of March the anniversary of the Sharpeville Massacre, a truly international day for the end of discrimination against the black community (CM/RES 102—IX), 1967).

In a resolution on Zimbabwe, the Council, further, urged the Members of the OAU, and other nations, to declare publicly that they would in no circumstances recognise any form of independence accorded to Zimbabwe by the principle of majority rule; and asked once again that those States increase their contributions to the OAU Special Fund for the liberation of Zimbabwe to enable the African nationalists to fight against the rebel regime in that area (CM/RES 108—IX, 1967).

The Council, therefore, recommended to the Executive Secretary of the Liberation Committee to extend financial aid and assistance desirable to the liberation movements of South Africa and Zimbabwe during the next year of activities of the OAU; and renewed its appeal to the liberation movements of Zimbabwe to exert fresh efforts to find a basis for unity, co-ordination and co-operation, for the constitution of a common front, in their struggle to liberate their country (Ibid).

By another resolution on Namibia, the Council stated that it supported unreservedly all the concrete measures taken by the Acting UN High Commissioner and the Council for Namibia (Konstantinos Stavropoulos of Greece) for setting up, as soon as possible, an international administration in the territory, to bring its mandate to a successful conclusion and hasten the accession of the people of Namibia to self-determination and independence. It reaffirmed the inalienable right of the people of that territory to freedom and independence by the OAU Charter, the UN Charter and other relevant resolutions, the 1960 Declaration on Independence in particular (CM/RES 110—IX, 1967).

At the following session, in February 1968, the Council adopted another set of resolutions on Zimbabwe, Portuguese-administered territories, South Africa, and Namibia, respectively. With the Zimbabwean resolution, the Council condemned: as a crime against humanity the atrocities perpetrated by the illegal racist minority regime in Rhodesia against the African people fighting for their freedom; the economic, financial and other interests which impeded the progress of the African people towards independence; and, unreservedly the Government of the UK for its continued failure in assuming effectively its moral and political responsibilities to the people of Zimbabwe and by allowing the 'illegal racist minority regime' of Ian Smith to consolidate its position in defiance of African and world opinion (CM/RES 135—X, 1968).

Furthermore, the Council strongly reiterated the Zimbabweans' right to freedom and independence, and again, appealed to the liberation movements of Zimbabwe to close their ranks and form a common front in their struggle against the common enemy for the speedy and effective liberation of their country (Ibid).

With the resolution on Portuguese Administered Territories, the Council also condemned, as a crime against humanity, the atrocities perpetrated by the Portuguese against the African people fighting for their freedom and independence; and the economic, financial, and other interests impeding the progress of the African people towards independence (CM/RES 137—X, 1968).

The Council, therefore, appealed to the International Monetary Fund (IMF) and International Bank for Reconstruction and Development (IBRD) not to grant aid to the Government of Portugal until that Government had recognised the right of the people under its domination to freedom and independence; and appealed, once more to all the independent African States to increase their material and moral support to the peoples of these territories in their struggle; the liberation movements to close their ranks in the struggle they were waging (Ibid).

In addition, the Council requested the Committee of Five for Angola to meet immediately to bring the MPLA and the Revolutionary Government of Angola in Exile (GRAE) together in a united front. In that connection, the Governments of the Republic of the Congo (Kinshasa) and Republic of the Congo (Brazzaville) were called upon to use their influence to secure the release – before the said meeting – of detainees held on either of their territories to promote an atmosphere of reconciliation and eventual peace between the two movements (Ibid).

By the one on Namibia, the Council, once again, unreservedly, condemned the Pretoria regime for its illegal and unjust action in arresting the 37 nationals of Namibian, in violation of the UN resolution terminating its mandate over South-West Africa and for subjecting the said South-West African citizens to its inhuman and racist laws (CM/Res 138—X, 1968). The 37 Namibian nationals included Andimba Herman Toivo ja Toivo, one of the founders of SWAPO, who was sentenced to 20 years imprisonment on Robben Island, off Cape Town's coast (South African History Online, https://www.sahistory.org.za).

The Council, therefore, demanded the immediate release of all Namibian patriots imprisoned for having fought for the liberation of their country, and urged the UN Security Council to do its utmost to secure the release of these prisoners following UN GA Resolution 2248 (S-V) of 19 May 1967 (CM/RES 138—X, 1968).

By CM/Res.142 (X), the Council, further, strongly reaffirmed the inalienable right of the people of the International Territory of South West Africa to freedom and independence in conformity with the Charter of the OAU, the UN Charter and the relevant resolutions of the OAU of the UN, particularly the 1960 Declaration on the Granting of Independence to Colonial Countries and Peoples: and its total and unflinching support to the people of South West Africa in their legitimate struggle (CM/RES 142—X, 1968).

Regarding racism and racial discrimination, the Council among other things: expressed its high esteem for all the sons and daughters of Southern Africa who were struggling tirelessly and bravely against apartheid and calls urgently upon all States to give them moral and material support in their struggle; and appealed to all States to observe the twenty-first of March, the anniversary of the Sharpeville Massacre (1960), as an international day for the abolition of racism (Ibid).

From September 4-12, 1968, the Council adopted resolutions on Namibia, Zimbabwe, and Portuguese oppression in Africa during its Eleventh Ordinary Session in Algiers, Algeria. With the one Namibia, the Council again, reaffirmed the right of the Namibian people to freedom and independence in conformity with the Charter of the OAU, and the UN; pledged again its total and unconditional support to the people of Namibia in their legitimate struggle; and appealed to the international community to render all moral and material assistance directly or through the OAU or the UN to those who were struggling against oppression in Namibia (CM/RES 150—XI, 1968).

By the one on Portuguese Administered Territories, the Council reaffirmed the legitimacy of the struggle waged by the peoples fighting against Portugal's colonial repression; condemned its persistent refusal to acknowledge the right to self-determination and independence of the peoples in the territories under its domination, in defiance of the UN resolutions; appealed to the Member States of the OAU to grant additional material assistance to the liberation movement to rebuild the economy and population; and, to all States to extend both moral and material assistance to those engaged in the legitimate struggle against Portuguese oppression in Africa (CM/RES 152—XI, 1968).

To that end, the Council congratulated the African nationalists on their progress in the legitimate struggle for the liberation of their countries; and called them to keep healthy and constructive relations with all Member States of the Organisation in the broader interest of the struggle which they were waging (Ibid).

With the resolution of Zimbabwe, the Council also strongly reaffirmed the right of the people of Zimbabwe to freedom and independence based on majority, and the legitimacy of their struggle for national liberation (CM/RES 153—XI, 1968).

The Council further requested OAU Member States to increase financial and material aid for the intensified struggle within Zimbabwe. It also appealed to all nations to provide moral and material assistance to the Zimbabwean people in their fight against colonial oppression (Ibid).

The Council also congratulated the freedom movements in Rhodesia for their efforts to counter the illegal regime and in particular ZAPU and ANC in creating a united front; and reaffirmed the resolution on decolonisation adopted by the International Conference of Human Rights, held at Teheran, Iran in 1968, and further reaffirms that since a state of war exists in Zimbabwe, that freedom fighters of Zimbabwe when captured be treated as prisoners of war under the International Red Cross Convention of 1949 (Ibid).

The Council, therefore, appealed once again to the liberation movement of Zimbabwe to close their ranks and form a united front and to this end requests the Governments of Tanzania, Zambia and Kenya to use their good offices with these movements; and instructed the African Group at the UN to work so that the SC Committee on the Question of Rhodesia could be reactivated to contribute effectively to the liberation of Zimbabwe (Ibid).

During its ordinary session, in February 1969, the Council adopted a Declaration on Decolonisation and Apartheid. This adoption stemmed from comprehensive information on the deteriorating situation in territories under colonial and racial domination. On Zimbabwe, in particular, the Council, took formal note of the efforts exerted by the African Heads of State and Government at the Commonwealth Ministers' Conference (January 1969) and deplored the negative attitude of the UK Government; and condemned and rejected the proposals of the UK Government, known as the "FEARLESS" proposals, which ran counter to the fundamental rights of the African population, strengthened the position of the white minority and encouraged the establishment of apartheid in Zimbabwe (CM/ST 2—XII, 1968).

The Council, further, reaffirmed that the future of Zimbabwe could not be negotiated with an illegal regime which had seized power in Zimbabwe; and, that the armed struggle was the only means of settling the Zimbabwean problem and denounced the manoeuvres of certain African opposition leaders who were trying to convince others that it was still possible to negotiate with the rebel regime of Ian Smith (Ibid).

It, therefore, appealed to the Member States to study the appropriate effective ways and means of rendering the armed struggle more effective, and to take appropriate steps to that end; and continued, it had been 'informed of the air transport agreement concluded between the Pretoria regime and the Government of the UK to ensure the release of that valiant freedom fighter and to ensure that Africans did not fall victims of those manoeuvres by the illegal Ian Smith regime' (Ibid).

Concerning Mozambique, the Council vehemently deplored the brutal assassination of Edwardo Mondlane (FRELIMO's first President). It appealed to the African populations in Mozambique to intensify their liberation struggle, demonstrating that Mondlane's sacrifice was not in vain (Ibid).

Once again, the Council stated that it had taken note with regret of the rift that existed between all liberation movements, and reiterated its appeal to the liberation movements, and in particular to FNLA and MPLA, to form a common front, which alone could guarantee final victory in their struggle. The Council also said that it had noted with satisfaction, 'the distinctly positive results attained by the PAIGC in Guinea-Bissau and encouraged it to redouble efforts for the total liberation of the territory (Ibid).

To that end, the Council condemned the growing military collaboration between Pretoria, Lisbon, and Salisbury, the increasing military collaboration between Pretoria, Lisbon, and Salisbury, recommending that Member States reconsider their approach to the liberation struggle in the remaining dependent territories (Ibid).

At its Thirteenth Ordinary Session, in September 1969, the Council adopted a resolution CM/RES 206—XIII, on Decolonisation and Apartheid. This adoption was based on the realisation of the difficulties and obstacles to be overcome in the successful conclusion of liberating Africa from foreign powers and racist and illegal regimes in Southern Africa. With Resolution CM/Res. 206 (XIII), the Council reaffirmed the legitimacy of the struggle launched in Zimbabwe, Mozambique, Angola, Guinea Bissau, Namibia, South Africa, Djibouti, Western Sahara and the Comoro Islands (CM/RES 206—XIII, 1969).

Based on the foregoing, the Council decided to submit the following recommendations to the Sixth Ordinary Session of the Assembly of Heads of State and Government: that all the liberation movements be required to form a common fighting front to achieve an early and speedy victory over the forces of oppression and exploitation; that no assistance be extended to liberation movements not recognised by OAU; that more substantial aid be extended to the liberation movements materially, financially and diplomatically; and that a new and well-conceived diplomatic and political offensive be launched by OAU Member States at all levels within international organisations to achieve the ultimate aim of the liberation of Africa (Ibid).

Concerned with the persistence of the racist regimes in South Africa, Namibia, Zimbabwe, and the Territories under Portuguese' intensive repression of African peoples and in thwarting their legitimate armed struggle, the Council took a step further, in March 1970, by adopting several other resolutions. For example, under the resolution on Zimbabwe, the Council reaffirmed its conviction that the use of force was the only way to restore the dignity of the people of Zimbabwe and decided to give immediate substantial additional assistance to the freedom fighters of Zimbabwe to help them intensify the armed struggle (CM/RES 207—XIV, 1970).

The Council, also urgently, appealed to the Member States of the OAU to take financial, material, military and other appropriate measures to meet the new situation; and paid tribute to those patriots of Zimbabwe engaged in armed struggle against the Salisbury illegal racist regime and called upon all the people of Zimbabwe to intensify the struggle for the liberation of their territory (Ibid).

The Council, once again, reaffirmed: that any form of military and other cooperation with those minority regimes constituted a hostile act against all African States and their peoples; and its full support for the liberation movements in Zimbabwe, Mozambique, Angola, Guinea Bissau, Namibia, South Africa, Djibouti, and the Comoro Islands against colonial rule (Ibid).

It, further appealed urgently to all Member States to increase their assistance to the liberation movements through the OAU; and to all States and Organisations supporting the liberation of the African continent to make contributions through the OAU for assistance to the people struggling against racism and colonialism and instructs the General Secretariat to make the necessary arrangements to receive such contributions (Ibid).

To that end, the Council commended the anti-apartheid movements and organisations of students, youth and others all over the world which had actively supported the struggle of the African peoples for liberation; and, further, appealed to all organisations and peoples in Africa to celebrate African Liberation Day on May 25, 1970, as widely as possible in full solidarity with the African peoples struggling against apartheid, colonialism and racial discrimination in the African continent and make racial discrimination in the African continent and make generous contributions for their legitimate struggle (Ibid).

The Council adopted another resolution at its subsequent followed up with another resolution at its next session in August 1970. Among other things, it congratulated the liberation movements in the territories under foreign domination for the success achieved in their valiant struggle for liberation and reaffirmed its full support (CM/RES 234—XV, 1970).

The Council adopted two resolutions at its 17th Ordinary Session in June 1971. The first was on Decolonisation, and the other was on Apartheid and Racial Discrimination. In a decolonization resolution, the Council commended the continued successes of liberation movements in foreign-dominated territories, particularly PAIGC, MPLA, FRELIMO and FNLA. It, therefore, urged those movements to intensify their struggle and appealed to the Member States of the

OAU to increase their assistance to those movements (CM/RES 241/REV.1—XVII, 1971).

The Council, also, appealed to friendly governments, organisations and individuals to contribute generously to the African liberation movements through the OAU, especially to enable them to carry on the urgent task of reconstruction in the liberated areas of Mozambique, Angola and Guinea Bissau; and expressed its appreciation to those governments, movements and organisations all over the world which supported the legitimate struggles of the African peoples against foreign domination, provide moral, political and material assistance to the liberation movements recognised by the OAU (Ibid).

It, therefore, commended the African Group at the UN for its efforts to promote more effective international action for decolonisation, and requested it to intensify these efforts, especially towards acceptance of liberation movements as authentic representatives of territories under colonial domination; and requested the General Secretariat to intensify publicity in favour of the liberation movements and against the governments and economic and financial interests collaborating with the colonial regimes in Africa, to secure support for the cause of the total emancipation of the continent (Ibid).

With the resolution on apartheid and racial discrimination, the Council, among other things, reaffirmed its full and unconditional support to the oppressed people of South Africa in their legitimate struggle to eliminate apartheid and achieve majority rule; commended the activities of all anti-apartheid movements and all Church, Trade Union, Students and other groups which supported the legitimate struggle of the oppressed people of Southern Africa and boycott South African racists (CM/RES 242/REV.1—XVII, 1971).

The Council also expressed its appreciation of the UN, anti-apartheid movements and other groups for their activities in supporting and the legitimisation of the liberation movements and called for continued efforts in that respect; and, appealed to all friendly Governments, organisations and individuals to extend increased moral, political, humanitarian and material support to the struggle of the people of South Africa, Namibia and Zimbabwe in cooperation with the OAU (Ibid).

To that end, it called for global campaigns to, among other things: apply the relevant articles of the 1949 Geneva Convention on prisoner of war treatment to freedom fighters and ensure the participation of liberation movements in drafting and applying international humanitarian law relevant to "internal conflicts" (Ibid).

At its Nineteenth Ordinary Session, the Council adopted resolutions on Zimbabwe, Portuguese colonies, Namibia, and on Apartheid and Racial Discrimination, respectively. These resolutions were approved by the OAU Assembly of Heads of State and Governments at its Ninth Session in 1972 (UN Digital Library, https://digitallibrary.un.org).

Under the resolution on Zimbabwe, the Council, among other things, pledged to increase its assistance to the people of Zimbabwe in their armed struggle for self-determination and independence; reaffirmed support for the principle that there should be no independence before majority rule in the territory (CM/RES 267—XIX, 1972).

The Council, therefore, appealed to the Government of the UK not to transfer or accord, under any circumstances, to the illegal regime any of the powers or attributes of sovereignty; and urged it to promote the country's attainment of independence by a democratic system of government following the majority of the population (Ibid).

Furthermore, the Council, urged the UK as an administering authority, to convene as soon as possible a national constitutional conference in which the guanine political representatives of the people of Zimbabwe would be able to work out a settlement relating to the future of the territory for subsequent endorsement by the people under free and democratic processes; and, appealed to the UK Government to create the conditions necessary to permit the free expression of the right to self-determination: including, among other things, the release of all political prisoners, detainees and restricted (Ibid).

To that end, it expressed among other things, full agreement with the proposal submitted by the delegations of Guinea, Somalia and Sudan, in their capacity as members of the UN SC, namely: that SC should reaffirm the inalienable rights of the people of Zimbabwe to freedom and independence in accordance with the Declaration on Independence, and the legitimacy of their struggle to secure the enjoyment of their rights as outlined in the UN Charter (Ibid).

By the one on Portuguese Administered Territories, the Council, among other things: solemnly reaffirmed the inalienable rights of the people of Angola, Mozambique and Guinea-Bissau to self-determination and independence; expressed its full support to the legitimate armed struggle of the people of those territories against colonist domination and oppression by Portugal for their freedom and independence; and also reaffirmed its commitment to pursue the struggle to total concerted effort and practical actions on the ground from various viewpoints and at all levels to liberate the territory (CM/RES 268—XIX, 1972).

The Council, therefore, appealed to the international community to recognise the liberation movements of the Portuguese colonies as the legitimate representatives of their peoples and countries and to discuss problems relating to those peoples and countries only with the liberation movements (Ibid).

The Council also encouraged all the national liberation movements of Angola, Mozambique, and Guinea-Bissau to intensify struggle against Portuguese colonialism and for national independence; decided to increase assistance to the liberation movements in those territories in conformity with the Liberation Committee's recommendation (Ibid).

The Council, further, invited the governments of OAU Member States to strengthen and increase their moral and material support for the liberation struggle being waged by the valiant freedom fighters of Angola, Mozambique, and Guinea-Bissau against Portuguese domination (Ibid).

With the one on Namibia it: reaffirmed the inalienable right of the people of Namibia to freedom and independence in one entity, in conformity with the 1960 UN Declaration on Independence; and reiterated its solidarity and full support to the people of Namibia in their just struggle to regain their freedom and independence (CM/RES 269—XIX, 1972).

The Council reaffirmed, further, that the administration of the territory of Namibia was the direct responsibility of the UN and that the responsibility included the obligation to support, promote and protect the rights of its inhabitants as well as national unity and territorial integrity of the state (Ibid).

With the resolution on Apartheid and Racial Discrimination, the Council, among other matters, appealed to the world community to render all moral, moral, material and financial assistance to the people of Namibia in their liberation struggle; and decided in accordance with the recommendation of the Liberation Committee to increase material support to SWAPO, to enable it to wage the armed struggle effectively in Namibia (CM/RES 270—XIX, 1972).

The Council also referred to in the text on Namibia, the question of the situation in South Africa. For instance, it paid tribute to the struggle of African people to regain their freedom and national independence. Secondly, it condemned the establishment of Bantustans and the forcible removal of the African people to those areas as a violation of their inalienable rights, contrary to the principle of self-determination and prejudicial to the territorial integrity of the countries and the unity of their peoples. Third, the Council reaffirmed the inalienable right of the African people of South Africa to self-determination and national independence within the framework of territorial integrity and national unity (Ibid).

The Council, further, reiterated its full and conditional support for the oppressed people of South Africa in their armed struggle to put an end to the policy of apartheid and realise their profound and legitimate aspirations; invited Member States to increase substantially moral and material aid to liberation movements in South Africa to hasten the elimination of the colonial and racist system in the country (Ibid).

Aside from support for the oppressed people, it rejected the South African authorities' attempt to break African solidarity and isolate the liberation movements through 'outward and dialogue' policies; and commended the activities of the anti-apartheid movements, trade unions, students' organisations, religious and other groupings which supported the legitimate struggle of the oppressed peoples of Africa and invited them to intensify their efforts in that respect (Ibid).

In May 1973, the Council adopted three resolutions concerning Zimbabwe, South Africa, and Namibia, and a Declaration on Portuguese-dominated territories. It reaffirmed its total and unconditional support for and solidarity with the people of Zimbabwe in their struggle for national independence based on majority rule. It noted with satisfaction the Lusaka Agreement between ZANU and ZAPU on the Strategy for the Liberation of Zimbabwe (CM/RES 298 (XXI, 1973).

By the same text, the Council also appealed to African states to further increase their material, financial and moral support to the national liberation movements of Zimbabwe either directly or through the OAU, and pledged support for and solidarity with all the front-line states, in particular Zambia. Accordingly, Zambians were subjected to constant economic and military provocations from the minority racist regimes of Southern Africa (CM/RES 299 (XXI, 1973).

Regarding South Africa, the Council reaffirmed its total and unconditional solidarity with its people in their legitimate struggle for national liberation; and pledged to increase its financial and material assistance to the struggle; and appealed to the liberation forces of South Africa to close ranks and form a united action against their common enemy (CM/RES 299 (XXI, 1973).

It, therefore, further expressed support to the initiative of the UN to organise in Geneva from 15- 17 June 1973, an International Conference of the Trade Unions against apartheid and appealed to all States and non-governmental organisations, including the All-African Trade Union Unity, to support and attend that Conference (Ibid).

Finally, the Council commended the actions of governments and organisations, including youth and sports organisations, which had refused to participate in sports activities with apartheid South Africa and requested them to further intensify their action in this respect (Ibid).

On the Namibian question, the Council, once again, reaffirmed its full support for its in their legitimate struggle for national independence and noted with satisfaction the positive development of the armed struggle waged by the Namibian people under the leadership of SWAPO; and appealed to the international community to increase its political, moral, financial, and other forms of support to the people of Namibia under the leadership of Namibia to enable them to conduct an effective armed struggle to expedite the attainment of independence of Namibia (C/RES 300—XXI, 1973).

With the declaration on the territories under Portuguese, the African States, among other things, decided to reinforce their moral and material support to the struggle for national liberation movements, either through the OAU or by stimulating bilateral aid, so that the liberation movements in the Portuguese colonies would be better able to deal with the gigantic tasks of armed struggle and national reconstruction (CM/ST 10—XXI, 1973).

The Assembly of African States decided to intensify public awareness of the armed struggle and its successes in Portuguese-dominated territories. This aims to foster total solidarity with the fighting peoples, considering the tasks facing the national liberation movement (Ibid).

At its Twenty-Third Ordinary Session, the Council adopted resolutions on South Africa and Namibia. With the resolution on South Africa and Namibia, the Council, reaffirmed its full unconditional support for the peoples of South Africa and Namibia in their legitimate struggle for national liberation; undertook to increase its financial and material assistance to the liberation movements of South Africa and Namibia given the imperative needs of the struggle; and, reiterated that the South African and Namibian liberation movements recognised by OAU were the authentic and legitimate representatives of the people of those territories (CM/RES 342 (XXIII, 1974).

As for Zimbabwe, the Council appealed to the country's patriots to take advantage of the situation in the territory and Southern Africa in general by increasing and intensifying action against the racist regime of Salisbury and to that end pledged increased assistance of every kind to the fighting forces of Zimbabwe to enable them increase and intensify their operations (Ibid).

The Council also appealed to the British Government to stop clandestine talks with Zimbabwe and urged all Zimbabweans to stand firm in a united demand for nothing less than majority rule and true self-government, and once again appealed to it as an administering power to bring about the necessary conditions to enable the Zimbabwean people to exercise freely their right to self-determination and independence (Ibid).

Once again, it appealed to the British Government to take appropriate measures for the unconditional release of all political prisoners, detainees and restricted, the repeal of all repressive and racist legislation, the expulsion of all South African forces from the territory and the convening of a constitutional conference in which the authentic representatives of the peoples would participate fully (Ibid).

In addition, the Council, requested the Administrative Secretary-General to organise a Seminar, in which the national liberation as well as African and other experts would participate, to consider the question of decolonisation, with particular emphasis on the key role played by South Africa in thwarting the liberation struggle in the country, and to report on the results of that Seminar to the 25th Session of the Council of Ministers. It, therefore, expressed its appreciation to all the peace and freedom-loving countries which had tirelessly lent their support to the struggle for decolonisation and appealed to them to increase their assistance in all fields to the peoples striving to liberate themselves from colonialism (Ibid).

In another action taken at the Twenty-Third Ordinary Session, the Council adopted a general resolution on Decolonisation, the Council reaffirmed once again, its total and unconditional support for the peoples under Portuguese, French, British and Spanish colonial domination in their legitimate struggle for national liberation; appealed to Portugal to proclaim unequivocally her recognition of the inalienable right of the people of Mozambique to independence; and, welcomed the talks between Portuguese authorities and the representatives of the Republic of Guinea-Bissau on the one hand, and the representatives of FRELIMO and Portugal on the other and encouraged the respective parties to continue the talks with the view to an early ending of the conflict (CM/Res.350—XXIII, 1974).

The Council, therefore, urged the national liberation movements to redouble their efforts and intensify their struggle in Angola and Mozambique until independence was achieved; and called upon expressly the national liberation of those territories, to take united action against their common enemies (Ibid).

During the same session, the Council further adopted a Declaration. The Assembly of Heads of State and Government endorsed this declaration at its eleventh session, held in Mogadishu, Somalia, Democratic Republic, in June 1974. Under the Declaration, the Council, among other things, declared that Africa gave its full support to the national liberation movements and their determination to fight until independence and total freedom of their peoples and countries of which they were the sole and authentic representatives; and, that Africa recalled that its stand was shared by the majority of the international community (*CM*/ST 13—XXVII, 1974). According to the Council, indeed, by its Resolution of 22 November 1972, it had called upon Portugal to immediately cease its military operations and acts of repression in African territories and enter negotiations with the liberation movements based on independence (Ibid).

The Council further noted with satisfaction that negotiations had already been held between the Republic of Guinea-Bissau led by the PAIGC and Portugal, as well as between FRELIMO and Portugal, and declared that the African position on the talks with Portugal was unqualifiedly supported by FRELIMO and the Republic of Guinea, led by the PAIGC. It, therefore, declared that to respect people's inalienable right to freedom and independence, Portugal should negotiate with the liberation movements recognised by the OAU. This was to transfer power to these movements as the legitimate representatives of their peoples and countries (Ibid).

To that end, the Council stated that Africa wishes to transfer its gratitude to all peace and freedom-supporting countries that have consistently aided national liberation in Africa, thereby contributing to resolving the colonial problem. Accordingly, while appreciating the efforts they were exerting in that connection, Africa appealed to them (freedom-loving countries) to bring stronger pressure to bear on Portugal to compel it to recognise the inalienable right of the people of African territories under its domination to freedom and independence (Ibid).

## 4.3 Conclusion

This chapter examines the OAU's role in representing national liberation movements at the UN. From the chapter's analysis, one finds that the organisation decided, from its inception, to assist and support the national liberation movements in Southern Africa. Critical to this aid and support, as observed, is OAU's diplomatic action on behalf of those movements. As discussed, this action's core was recognising national liberation movements as the authentic representatives of people's aspirations in colonial territories. It was noted that the Executive Council (Council of Ministers and the Assembly of Heads of State and Government)'s decisions, especially those adopted during the period between 1963 and 1974, revealed the extent of OAU support and assistance to the movements. The chapter concludes that, analysed at the diplomatic level, the OAU Executive Council's decisions contributed to the national liberation movements' representation at the UN. The next chapter discusses the effects for representation of national liberation movements at the UN.

# CHAPTER FIVE

## The Effects of Representation of National Liberation Movements at the UN

### 5.1 Introduction

This chapter concerns the effects of representation of national liberation movements at the UN. It is divided into three sections. Section one introduces the subject. The next section discusses the effects of national liberation representation at the UN. It explores, as case examples, the First Session of the UN IHL (1974); the UN Conference on the Representation of State Relations with International Organisations (1975); and the World Conference on International Women's Year (1975), to describe those effects. The last section is a conclusion.

When the UN was formed in 1945, the peoples of non-self-governing or non-dependent territories were regarded as 'minors' within the jurisdiction of the administering power and not entitled to a separate representation. In some international organisations, non-independent territories were permitted separate representation (Shaw, 1983). Article 73 of Chapter XI of the UN Charter obliged the administering powers to recognise the interests and well-being of the peoples whose territories had not yet attained a full measure of self-government (ICJ, https://popp.undp.org).

The next stage involved the characterisation of what could generally be regarded as 'prototype' liberation movements as petitioners within the UN framework. The petition approach did not satisfy the UN membership because of the Trusteeship Council's failure to process the petitions (Terretta, 2012). The petition scheme was originally part of the trusteeship system but was in fact extended beyond this to relate to colonial territories in general. The hearing of such petitions was discretionary, and the petitioners themselves participated as private individuals and not as representatives of organisations. For example, in 1946, the ANC President, A.B. Xuma, through the Indian delegation, lobbied privately at the UN GA (Shaw, 1983) on the question of race relations in South Africa. The examination of these petitions was done by an ad hoc committee, established by the Trusteeship Council in March 1950 (UN, 1950).

The third phase in the efforts to secure the participation of the liberation movements in the UN took place between 1972 and 1973 when the GA's Fourth Committee and the Special Committee on Independence invited representatives of the national liberation movements to participate as observers in debates relating to their territories. During this phase, the UN affirmed for the first time that the national liberation movements were the "authentic representatives" of the aspirations of the people in their territories. The world body also urged all Member States and specialised agencies within the UN system to engage the national liberation movements, in consultation with the OAU, when dealing with territorial matters (Trevona, 2007). The OAU was consulted to screen and exclude secessionist movements from UN participation, ensuring only OAU-recognised national liberation movements benefitted from the world body (Shaw, 1983).

The liberation movements' participation in observer status was then followed in 1974 by "regular participation" at the UN when the GA decided to invite personnel from the liberation movements to participate in conferences, seminars, and other meetings held under the UN auspices (UN, 1975).

**Diagram 2**: Stages for the representation of national liberation movements in the UN

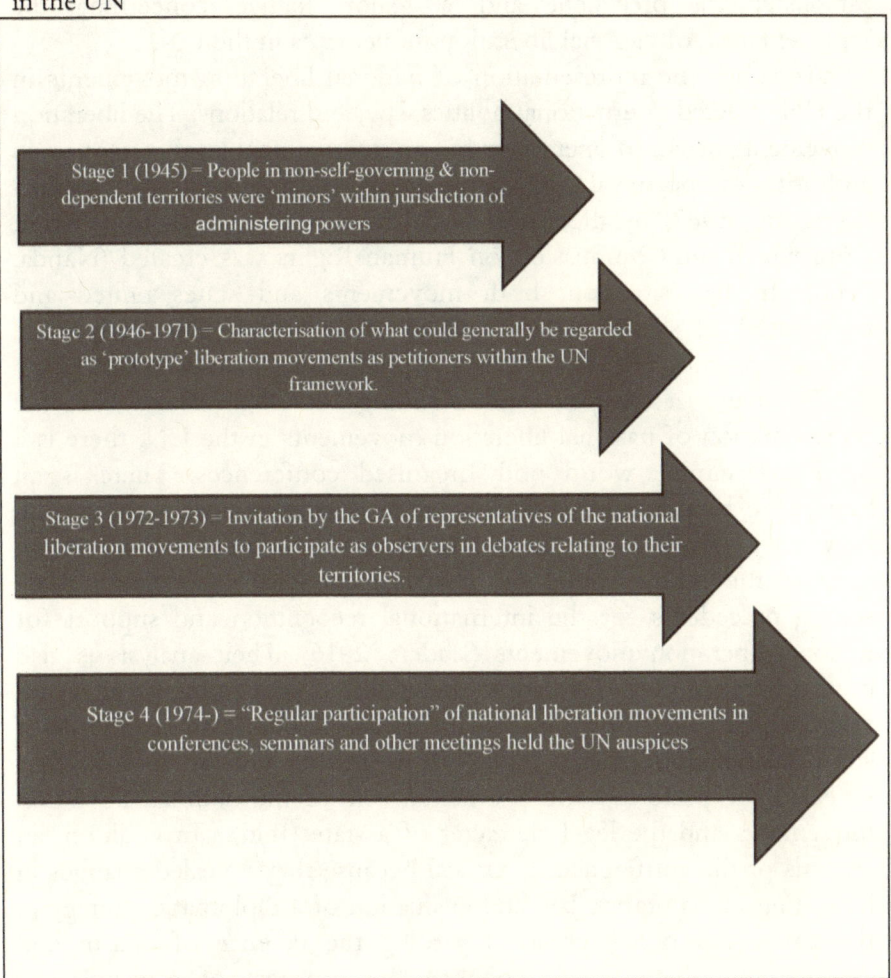

The Western nations opposed the movements' participation in the international conferences. For instance, the United States of America (USA) and several countries from western Europe argued that their participation would hinder efforts towards advancing human rights in an armed conflict (Shaw, 1983). The argument was that these organisations lacked a basis for participating in conferences formulating new international law concepts, as none had gained international recognition as legitimate representatives of an established state (Graham, 1975). Later, the internal rules of the conferences were amended to permit the liberation movements to participate, thereby establishing a precedent and a major change concerning the representation of national liberation movements in the UN.

Arguably, the representation of national liberation movements in the UN affected international politics, law, and relations. The liberation movements began to operate within an international legal system or an authority—a portrayal of enforcement of human rights norms (D'Amato, 1982) by the world body in accordance with its Charter, from which the Commission on Human Rights was created (Nanda, 2006). In this situation, both movements and states united and cooperated in signing treaty relations that limited their respective powers, an action with significant political impact (Wibowo, 2021).

To have a deeper understanding of the effects of the representation of national liberation movements in the UN, there is a need to examine world body-organised conferences. There is an imperative to examine those that were organised during the period between 1974 and 1975. An analysis of these conferences is important because they consolidated the challenge to state sovereignty, while setting precedents for the international recognition and support for national liberation movements (Ludert, 2016). Their analysis is also critical because they revealed several political developments in recent years, which have thrown into sharp focus the relevance of the rule of self-determination (Asmal, 1984). It is further critical because they revealed the preferred and protracted role of the national liberation movements and the legal character of a state (Ibid). In addition, an analysis of the conferences is critical because they revealed changes in legislating humanitarian law and evaluation of a diplomatic strategy in the light of a policy choice regarding the defence of racism and colonialism, which would enhance the prospect of effective law (Forsythe, 1975).

## 5.2 Effects of the Representation of National Liberation Movements at the UN

### 5.2.1 The First Session of the Diplomatic Conference on the Reaffirmation and Development of IHL Applicable in Armed Conflicts

This Conference was held from 20 February to 29 March 1974 in Geneva, Switzerland (OR DCRD IHL, 1978). It was the first full-fledged diplomatic conference in 25 years to create new law for the protection of war victims (Forsythe, 1975). The Conference was also the first in 40 years to take up the question of restricting the use of conventional weapons. It was also the first extensive examination since World War I of attack methods and their impact on the civilian population (Ibid).

The conference primarily debated the status of national liberation movements, specifically those in Southern Africa and the Palestinian Liberation Organisation (PLO). This debate had the most remarkable results both for national liberation movements and for the history of international laws (Pillay, 2000).

The preparations for the session began in 1965. The Diplomatic Conference opened on 20 February 1974 with a statement by Pierre Graber, former Vice-President of the Swiss Federal Council and Head of the Swiss Federal Political Department, in his capacity as Acting President. Andre Chavanne, former Vice-President of the State Council of the Republic and Canton of Geneva, Vittorio Winspeare Guicciardi, former Director-General of the UN Office at Geneva and representative of the Secretary-General of the UN at the Conference; as well as, Eric Martin, former President of the ICRC, also made statements at the opening meeting (DCRD IHL, 1974).

The opening meeting of the Conference was closed by a statement from Mokhtar Ould Dada, President of the Islamic Republic of Mauritania. Held at the invitation of the Swiss Federal Council, the object of the session was to study two draft Additional Protocols prepared, after official and private consultations, by the ICRC and intended to supplement the four Geneva Conventions of 12 August 1949 (Ibid).

Those Protocols were Geneva Convention for the Amelioration of the Condition of the Wounded and Sick in Armed Forces in the Field (I); Geneva Convention for the Amelioration of the Condition of Wounded, Sick and Shipwrecked Members of Armed Forces at Sea (II); Geneva Convention relative to the Treatment of Prisoners of War (III); and the Geneva Convention relative to the Protection of Civilian Persons in Time of War [IV] (Forsythe, 1975).

One hundred and twenty-six (126) states were represented at this session. The largest delegation was that of the United States, consisting of twenty-six (26) persons, drawn from the Department of State and Defence (Barker, 1975; Graham, 1975). The invitation was also sent to national liberation movements recognised by regional intergovernmental organisations. This was given the importance of ensuring broad participation in the work of the Conference, which was fundamentally humanitarian. This was also due to the recognition that national liberation movements could positively contribute to the progressive development and codification of international humanitarian law applicable in armed conflicts, a universal task (DCRD IHL, 1974).

The following national liberation movements accepted the invitation and were represented at the first session of the Conference: PLO; FRELIMO; MPLA; FNLA, ANC (South Africa); PAC (South Africa); ZAFU; ZANU; SWAPO; Somali Coast Liberation Front (FLCS); Djibouti Liberation Movement (MLD); Seychelles People's United Party (SPUP); San Tome and Principe Liberation Movement (MLSTP); and the Comoros National Liberation Movement (MOLINACO] (DCRD IHL, 1974).

For the first time, the national liberation movements used the Diplomatic Conference, which was officially open to them to push for a larger conceptual understanding of superfluous injury and unnecessary suffering to hold imperialism and imperial states accountable for suffering and injury beyond that of physical death or wounding and to recognise the violence of colonisation and the social and cultural destruction it brought (Kinsella, 2017). The national liberation movements participated fully in the deliberations of the Diplomatic Conference and its Main Committees. Their participation in the Conference also illuminated a moment when "the natural order of domination was interrupted by the institution of a part of those who have no part" (Ibid). This implied that the movements' participation neutralised the decision-making process which was government representatives.

The statements or proposals, and amendments made or submitted by delegations of the national liberation movements were circulated by the Conference Secretariat as Conference documents to all participants in the Conference. However, it was understood that only delegations representing states were entitled to vote. Several organisations with observer status within the UN were also represented at the Conference (Barker, 1975). The Working Group for the Development of Humanitarian Law, which comprised several intergovernmental and non-governmental organisations also participated. The ICRC, which had prepared the two draft Additional Protocols, participated in the work of the Conference in an expert capacity (DCRD IHL, 1978).

The question of participation and representation opened with a 'bang' in the form of a speech by President Ould Dada of the Islamic Republic of Mauritania, who came strongly against the 'Zionists', Rhodesia, South Africa, and Portugal, and in favour of national liberation movements, and freedom fighters generally (Ibid). Dada's statement set the tone for the Session, which the Third World countries saw as an opportunity to change the status of the national liberation movements (Alexander, 2016). Due to Dada's statement, the session was slowed down by an unexpected virulent political debate. In fact, the Third World countries demanded full participation for national liberation movements in the Session, with or without voting rights, rather than mere observer status. However, the United States and other countries of the Western European group engaged in energetic efforts to block the invitation of the national liberation movements. But the situation calmed because of the affirmative vote on the participation of the national liberation movements (Barxter, 2013).

Although the national liberation movements were not formally permitted to vote in the Diplomatic Conference, their contributions had the authority and force of the official documents. The liberation movements would later be invited to sign the Final Act of the Conference, an indication of the renegotiation and transformation of the politics of law-making over the years of meetings (Kinseller, 2017).

The Conference's plenary meeting commenced on 20 February 1974. After electing Pierre Grabler, then Federal Councillor and Vice President of the Swiss Federal Council, President of the Conference, the Conference held no further official meeting until 27 February (DCRD IHL, 1978).

By the practice followed by major diplomatic conferences, the geographical groups (Africa, Latin America, West European and other States, and the East European States) had several informal consultations with the Presidency. It was these informal consultations with the Presidency that helped the Conference in reaching an agreement on several points. The purpose of the informal consultations was to deal with the major obstacles facing the Conference, including, *inter alia*, concerned the question of extending invitations to participants, the distribution of official posts, and the rules of procedure (Graham, 1975).

As a result, on 28 February 1974, the Conference admitted Guinea-Bissau by consensus to participate in the official meetings, which had resumed to discuss participation. Because of the failure to reach an agreement on the participation of the Provisional Revolutionary Government of the Republic of South Vietnam (PRG), the Conference decided to vote on the matter. It refused to invite that Government by a vote of 38 to 37 (DCRD IHL, 1978).

On 1 March 1974, the Conference, also by consensus, granted the national liberation movements recognised by the OAU and the LAS the right to participate in the Conference's proceedings. However, the movements were not allowed to vote. This was based on the understanding that only delegations representing States or governments would be entitled to vote. The decision to grant the national liberation movements the right to participate in the Conference was in pursuance of the resolutions adopted by the XXIInd International Conference of the Red Cross, held in Tehran, during the twenty-eighth session of the UN GA. Specifically, these resolutions urged the Diplomatic Conference to consider inviting such liberation movements (Graham, 1975).

At the same time, the Conference confirmed by consensus that an agreement had been reached on the distribution of official posts, namely the appointment of the Vice-Presidents of the Conference, and the Chairmen, Vice-Chairmen, and Rapporteurs of the four main Committees, the Drafting Committee, and the Credentials Committee (DCRD IHL, 1978). This phase of the proceedings ended with the Conference's approval of the Committee's program of work and adoption of the rules of procedure, based on the report drawn up by the Drafting Committee, chaired by Sayed Chowdhury (Bangladesh), on several proposed amendments to the draft rules of procedure (Ibid).

From 5 to 11 March 1974, during the initial plenary meetings devoted to general discussion, delegates stated their position regarding the draft Protocols Additional to the Geneva Conventions. Most of the delegates expressed the view that the Geneva Conventions and other questions relating to the application of humanitarian law were interesting issues for discussion at the Conference (Ibid).

On 11 March, three of the four main Committees began to deal with the draft Protocols Additional to the Geneva Conventions submitted by the ICRC. Committee II, unlike the other committees, had started its meetings on 6 March, during the plenary meetings. The last of Committee II's meetings was held on March 21, 1974 (Ibid).

One of the results of the Committee II's meetings was the approval of an amendment to the draft article defining the scope of the Protocol applicable in international armed conflicts, and its inclusion in the field of application of Protocol I and the Geneva Conventions (UN, 1974). Specifically, Article 1 of the Protocol—General principles included, among other things, armed conflicts in which people were fighting against colonial and alien occupation and racist regimes in the exercise of their right of self-determination, as enshrined in the Charter of the UN and Declaration of Principles of International Law concerning Friendly Relations and Co-operation among States by the Charter of the UN A/RES 2625—XXV, 1970).

Committee II chaired by T. Mallik of Poland with D. Maiga of Mali as rapporteur, was concerned with the protection of the wounded, the sick, and the shipwrecked, as well as with health transport, civil defence bodies, and relief. It also had a Drafting Committee chaired by B. Jakovljevic of former Yugoslavia, and a Technical Sub-Committee on Signs and Signalling, chaired by H.A. Kieffer, a Swiss expert (DCRD IHL, 1978).

The purpose of the Sub-Committee was to study the rules relating to the identification and marking of medical and civil defence personnel, units, and vehicles and draft Protocols Addition to the Geneva Conventions put forward by the IRC, concerning improved signalling and identification, and hence protection, for medical services and civil defence (Ibid). The Drafting Committee was responsible for coordinating and reviewing the drafting of all the texts adopted by the Main Committees (Ibid).

Chaired by E. Hambro of Norway, Committee I opened the discussion on general provisions and applications. One of the questions that arose in the Committee related to the national liberation wars (Ibid). This issue was discussed, and a report thereof was adopted at the final plenary meeting. It showed that the essential provision discussed by Committee I was Article I of draft Protocol I, also considered in a working group chaired by Miguel Marin-Bosch [Mexico] (Ibid).

Committee I also examined Article 2 (Definitions), Article 3 (Beginning and end of the application), Article 4 (Legal Status of the Parties to the conflict), and Article 5 (Appointment of Protecting Powers and their substitute). After examining the articles, the Committee proposed amendments to about fifteen articles in Draft Protocol II, applicable in non-international armed conflicts, but could not discuss them in the first session due a to lack of time (Ibid).

Committee III was chaired by H. Sultan (Egypt) and presided over by its rapporteur, R. Baxter of the United States of America (USA). Its purpose was to examine the problem imperfectly covered by international humanitarian law— the protection of the civilian population against hostilities. Committee III was also partly tasked with Articles 44 and 26 of draft Protocols I and II, respectively, concerning the field of application of the rules (Ibid).

One result of the Committee's meetings was the adoption, though with reservations, of the field of application of the Protocols, Articles 43 and 45 of Protocol II and the corresponding articles (Articles 23 and 25), on the protection and definition of the civilian population. The Committee, however, could not reach an agreement as to whether the Protocols should cover the protection of civilians on land alone or even in the air (e.g., civilian aircraft) and at sea (e.g., in merchant's vessels), and also failed to discuss numerous amendments submitted to various articles in the Protocols In addition to the three main Committees, the Conference decided by sixty-eight votes to none, with ten abstentions, to constitute an Ad Hoc Committee of the Whole on Conventional Weapons. It was chaired by D. Garces (Colombia), with F. Kalshoven (Netherlands) as a rapporteur (Ibid).

The constitution of the Ad Hoc Committee was pursuant to the ICRC's meeting of experts convened in Geneva (1973) and resolutions adopted by the XXIInd International Conference of the Red Cross (Tehran, November 1973), and the twenty-eighth session of the UN GA. The mandate of the Ad Hoc Committee was to examine the question of prohibition or restriction of the use of specific categories of conventional weapons which might cause unnecessary suffering or have indiscriminate effects (e.g., napalm, pellet bombs and dum-dum bullets) and consider all proposals which are submitted to the Conference relating to such weapons (Ibid).

One outcome of the Ad Hoc Committee of the Whole on Conventional Weapons' meetings was the adoption of a work plan on weapons, as proposed by the ICRC. The plan included, among other things, the convening of a Conference of Government Experts by the ICRC (ICRC, 1974).

On 28 and 29 March 1974, at its final plenary meetings, the Conference studied and noted reports of its committees. Given the importance of Committee I's report, the Conference adopted, by consensus, a resolution on the proposal of India (UN, 1974). By this text, the Conference welcomed the report of Committee I, particularly the adoption of Article I of the draft Protocol. The article's adoption was a declaration that wars of national liberation were on an equal footing with international armed conflicts (Verhoeven, 2007).

As a follow-up, President Graber pointed out at the final plenary meeting that the Diplomatic Conference had not concluded but suspended its work. It was therefore decided to hold a second session in Geneva, from 3 February to mid-April 1975 (UN, 1974).

The Conference, under a resolution submitted by: Bangladesh; Canada; Egypt; India; Mexico; Nigeria; Sri Lanka; Sudan; Sweden; and Yugoslavia, invited the participants to submit amendments and proposals on the draft Protocols, if possible before 15 September 1974, for the Secretariat of the Conference to distribute before 15 November (Ibid).

The next section concerns the UN Conference on the Representation of States' Relations with International Organisations. This Conference is significant because, to achieve common interests, States and their representatives develop international organisations (Nurhartano, 2023), and the UN is one such organisation.

### 5.2.2 *United Nations Conference on the Representation of States' Relations with International Organisations*

From 4 February to 14 March 1975, the UN convened a conference entitled 'The United Nations Conferences on Representation of States relations with International Organisations' in Vienna, Austria. It was the seventh UN GA Conference called to draw up, international conventions embodying the efforts of the world community to comply with the task, laid down in the Charter, of 'encouraging the progressive development of international law and its codification to strengthen the legal basis for international cooperation and full realisation of international détente (UN, 1976).

The Conference was held under the GA Resolution 3272—XXVII of 30 November 1973. By this resolution, the Assembly had decided, inter alia, that the UN Conference on the Representation of States in Their Relations with International Organisation would be held early in 1975 in Vienna (A/RES 3272—XXVII, 1973). Also, the Assembly had, by the same resolution, referred to the Conference, as a basic proposal for its consideration, draft articles adopted by the International Law Commission [ILC] (Ibid).

The ILC had, in 1958, brought the attention of the UN GA to the question of relations between states and international organisations. At the invitation of the GA, the ICL had placed the question on its agenda for its 1963 session (UN CRSIO, 1976). The Assembly, then appointed Judge Abdullah El-Erian of Egypt as Special Rapporteur and requested him to submit a report on 'relations between states and intergovernmental organisations, who also acted as an expert consultant to the conference (Ibid).

In recent years, the Special Rapporteur has drafted several reports and working papers. In 1969, he submitted a full set of draft articles with commentaries on the legal position of representatives of states to international organisations. After discussion and amendment by the ILC, those drafts were submitted to governments for comments. Considering those comments, the ILC completed its final draft of the articles in 1971 (Ibid, 1975).

Once again, the GA invited the Governments to comment on the final ILC draft articles. At its twenty-seventh session, the Assembly by Resolution 2966—XXVII of 14 December 1972, decided to convene an international conference of plenipotentiaries. The idea was to consider the question of the representation of states in their relations with international organisations and, using the ILC draft articles as a basis, to embody the results of its work in an international convention and such other instruments as might have been deemed appropriate (A/RES 2966—XXVII, 1972).

In its twenty-ninth session in 1974, the GA decided to determine at its twenty-ninth session (in 1974) the question of participation in the Conference. This item was included in its agenda on 21 September 1974 and allocated to the Sixth (Legal) Committee (UN YB, 1974).

On the recommendation of the Sixth Committee, the Assembly decided to invite all States to participate in the UN Conference on the Representation of States in Their Relations with International

Organisations, and to invite also the national liberation movements recognised by the OAU and/or the League of Arab States (LAS) in their respective regions to participate in the Conference as observers, by the practice of the UN (Ibid).

In response to the invitation by the Government of Austria, the GA subsequently decided, by a resolution 3072—XXVIII of 30 November 1973, that the conference be held in Vienna early in 1975. On 29 November 1974, the Assembly invited all states to participate in the Conference, and by that decision, eighty-one States attended the Conference. The governments of Iran and Iraq were represented by observers (UN YB, 1974).

The GA also requested the specialised agencies, International Atomic Energy Agency (IAEA), and relevant intergovernmental organisations to send observers to the conference. Thus, the following intergovernmental organisations accepted the invitation and were represented by observers at the Conference: ILO, FAO, UNESCO, WHO, and IAEA. Other intergovernmental organisations attending included the Council of Europe (COE), the European Economic Community, and the LARS (Ibid).

By Resolution 3247—XXIX of 29 November 1974, the GA decided to invite also the national liberation movements recognised by the OAU and/or by the LAS in their respective regions to participate in the Conference as observers. Thus, the following national liberation movements accepted that invitation and were represented by observers at the Conference: the Movement for the National Liberation of Comoro (MNLC); FNLA; PLO; PAC; MPLA; SWAPO; and the ZAPU (A/RES 3247—XXIX, 1974).

The Conference on the Representation of States in Their Relations with International Organisations opened on 4 February 1975, with a statement by Erik Suy, Legal Counsel of the UN, on behalf of the Secretary-General. Rudolph Kirchschlaeger, President of the Federal Republic of Austria, also made a statement at the opening meeting. Jose Sette Camara (Brazil), a prominent international lawyer, diplomat, and Brazil's permanent representative at the UN, was nominated as the Conference President (UN CRSIO, 1975).

In his statement, Suy, among other things, re-stated the purpose of the Conference as 'to examine the ILC's draft articles on the representation of State relations with international organisations and to include the results of its work in an internationally binding convention'. As Kirchschlaeger noted, the Conference's subject matter expressed the growing recognition of the importance of international organisations (Ibid).

The basis for the work of the Conference was the draft articles prepared by the ILC at its fourteenth session in 1962. These comprised eighty-two articles covering all aspects of the existing relations between States and international organisations. In addition, the Conference considered the twenty-four articles that dealt with observer delegations to organs and conferences (Ibid).

Most importantly, the Conference would undertake the historic step of establishing rules to govern relations between states and international organisations, to define in clear-cut terms the status of the representatives of States to international organisations, to assure them of complete parity with traditional diplomatic agents (UN CRSIO, 1975).

On 5 February, at its third plenary meeting, the Conference nominated Vice Presidents according to regional groupings (Africa, Asia, Eastern, and Western Europe). The Conference also elected Nettel (Austria) as Chairperson of the Committee of the Whole by acclamation (Ibid).

The nominees for the position of Vice-Presidents were Bulgaria; Chile; Egypt; France; India; Italy; Japan; Lebanon; Liberia; Libyan Arab Republic; Malaysia; Mali; Madagascar; Mexico; Netherlands; Panama; Union of Soviet Socialist Republics (USSR); UK; United States of America (USA); Venezuela; and former Yugoslavia (Ibid).

The Conference also set up four committees and a Secretariat. Those committees were: the General Committee, the Committee of the Whole, the Drafting Committee, and the Credentials Committee. The *General Committee* was chaired by the President of the Conference. Its members were the President and Vice Presidents of the Conference, the Chairperson of the Committee of the Whole, and the Chairperson of the Drafting Committee (UN CRSIO, 1976).

The *Committee of the Whole* was Chaired by Erik Nettel of Austria. Its members were: Max Wershof of Canada and Alfons Klafkowski of Poland. The *Drafting Committee* was chaired by Solomon Sogbetun of Nigeria. Its members were: the Chairperson of the Drafting Committee, from Argentina, France, Iraq, Morocco, Netherlands, Pakistan, Peru, Switzerland, USSR, UK, Tanzania, US, and an ex officio, by the rules of procedure of the Conference and Rapporteur of the Committee of the Whole (Ibid).

The *Credentials Committee* was chaired by Jose Plana of the Philippines, and the members were from Belgium, Ecuador, Guatemala, Hungary, Ivory Coast, Philippines, Thailand, Cameroon, and the US. This Committee met on 6 March 1975 to formalise invitations and credentials for participation, as well as the lists of representatives participating in the Conference (Ibid).

The Secretariat of the Conference was composed of the representatives of the Secretary-General of the UN, Under-Secretary-General, the Legal Counsel, Erik Suy; Executive Secretary of the Conference, Director of the Codification Division, Yuri M. Rybakov; Secretary of the Committee of the Whole, N. Teslenko, Assistant Secretaries of the Committee of the Whole, J. Dauchy and R. Zacklin; Secretary of the Drafting Committee, S. Torres Bernardez; Deputy Secretaries of the Drafting Committee, E. Valencia Ospina; and R. Sommereyns (Ibid).

By its rules of procedure, adopted on 4 February 1975, the Conference assigned to the Committee of the Whole the consideration of the draft articles on the representation of States in their relations with international organisations adopted by the ILC (Ibid).

Beyond drafting, coordinating, and reviewing adopted texts, the Drafting Committee was tasked by the Conference with preparing the title, preamble, and final clauses of the Convention, and the Final Act of the Conference (Ibid).

At its 5th plenary meeting, on 20 February 1975, the Committee of the Whole approved the draft articles on the representation of States in their relations with international organisations. The approval of the draft articles was based on the proposal submitted by Bulgaria, Byelorussian SSR, Cuba, Czechoslovakia, Germany, Hungary, Mongolia, Poland, Ukrainian SSR, and the USSR. The articles concerned delegations to organs and conferences, as well as observer delegations to organs and conferences (Ibid).

On 11 March 1975, the President expressed his gratitude to the Chairman and Rapporteur of the Committee of the Whole and the Chairman of the Drafting Committee for their work; and reminded the Conference to conclude its work in time for the Convention and Final Act thereof, to be ready for signature on 14 March (UN CRSIO, 1975).

To that end, the President proposed that the proceedings be conducted by the rules of the procedure whereby delegations would confine themselves to one statement not exceeding three minutes, including an explanation of vote, on any one article; and urged that the Conference complete its first consideration of the draft articles of the Convention before taking up any draft (Ibid).

Based on the foregoing, the Conference approved the titles and texts of articles adopted by the Committee of the Whole. Two days later, the Conference adopted, by a vote of fifty-seven in favour to one against, with fifteen abstentions (Fennessey, 1976), the Vienna Convention on the Representation of States in Their Relations with International Organisations of a Universal Character (Vienna Convention, 1975).

The most noticeable feature of the Convention was the high level of privileges and immunities accorded to the representatives [delegations] (Fennessey, 1976). It was, accordingly, hailed as the latest in a series of treaties that had resulted from the work of the ILC, and one of the treaties had been designed to codify and develop the principles of diplomatic relations (Ibid). It was also hailed as one of the major codifying treaties concluded under UN auspices (Brazil, 1975). Its language reflected the historical and geopolitical landscape that existed in the 1960s—one in which the pace of immigration was at a relative lull and Cold War spy games, not state-level capital offences were a top priority (Howell, 2013).

What distinguished the 1975 Convention from its predecessors (1961 and 1963 Conventions on Diplomatic and Consular Relations and the 1969 Convention on Special Missions) was that it seemed unlikely to attract the support of a substantial number of states most affected by its provisions—the major host states for international organisations (Fennessey, 1976).

In the vote adopting the Convention, Belgium's "no" vote highlighted that distinction. The abstaining states included the US (host state for the UN), Switzerland, and host states for various UN organs (ILO, WHO, UP, etc.): Austria (host state for IAEA and UNIDO), Canada (host state for International Civil Aviation Organisation [ICAO]), France (host state for UNESCO), and the UK (host state for Inter-governmental Maritime Consultative Organisation [IMCO]) (Ibid).

Generally, *the Vienna Convention on the Representation of States in Their Relations with International Organisations of a Universal Character*, as a whole, would serve as the basis for regulating the posting of State representatives in relation to international organisations of a universal character. The Convention would also be important in providing special protection to states' representatives posted elsewhere—thereby strengthening collaboration with international organisations that opened or established permanent secretariats or branch offices around the world (Vienna Convention, 1975).

In addition to the Convention, the Conference also adopted a Final Act and five accompanying resolutions. One of these resolutions was introduced directly after the plenary, related to the status of the liberation movements recognised by the OAU and/or the LAS (AJoIL, 1975).

The Conference, in its resolution on the status of liberation movements, requested the UN General Assembly during its 1975 regular session to ensure national liberation movements could effectively participate as observers in international organisations (UN CRSIO, 1975).

By another resolution, relating to the application of the Convention in future activities of international organisations, the Conference recommended to the Assembly of the UN that a suitable request should be made to the Secretary-General to inform the Member States that had asked for boats of future international organisations of a universal character or conferences convened by, or under the auspices of international organisations of a universal had duly ratified or had acceded to the Vienna Convention or Representation of States in Their Relations with International Organisations of a universal character (UN YB, 1976).

The remaining resolutions introduced directly in the plenary of the Conference were adopted by acclamation. With these resolutions, the Conference resolved to express gratitude and appreciation to Abdulla El-Erian, the expert consultant for the conference, and the ILC for their contribution to the codification and progressive development of the rules of international law, and the Government and inhabitants of Austria for their contribution to the successful completion of the performance of the conference (UN CRSIO, 1975).

The Final Act was signed on 14 March 1975, and the Convention, subject to ratification, was open for signature and for accession on that date. After 30 September 1975, the Convention was deposited with the Secretary-General of the UN (Ibid).

The Conference, therefore, recommended that the states concerned, in the meantime, accord to the delegations of the liberation movements concerned the necessary facilities, privileges, and immunities; and they should also be guided therein by the provisions of the Conventions (UN YB, 1976).

The next section is about the World Conference on International Women's Year. This Conference is important because it allowed women leaders from national liberation movements, particularly in Southern Africa, to mutually advocate for their right to political power (Ford Library).

*5.2.3  The World Conference on International Women's Year*

In 1975, the UN held the World Conference on International Women's Year in Mexico City. This Conference was hailed as 'the capstone event' of International Women's Year, the UN's response to the transnational women's liberation movement sweeping the globe (Olcott, 2017). Even though it could not be called a women's conference–since official participants were governments—it was the first intergovernmental meeting, where women formed part of virtually every delegation (UN Audiovisual Library, https://unmultimedia.org). Accordingly, it was also the first to show or reveal women's political agency during the Cold War era, which took different forms, including the refusal and the acceptance of women's activism within existing national and international institutions (Bonfiglioli, 2016).

The Conference would pay attention to matters such as 'political decision making, educational opportunities, economic opportunities, a different status in civil courts and all questions of maternity' (Ruto, 2009). Importantly, the Mexico City meeting would also recommend to the GA the idea of launching the 'United Nations Women's Decade: 1975-1985' and a convening of a world conference to review mid-term the progress made in implementing the objectives of Mexico and adjust as necessary (Ibid).

The Women's Conference was born out of pressures from the Women's movement in the US, and to a certain extent in the UK and West Germany (Godsee, 2012). Its purpose was: to promote equality between men and women; ensure the full participation of women in the total development effort; and recognise the importance of increasing the contribution of women to the development of friendly relations among states, to strengthen peace (McDougal, Lasswell & Chen, 1975).

The Conference had 133 government representatives, 113 of whom were women. One hundred and thirteen of these delegations were women. Representatives from the UN Secretariat, other UN bodies, and specialised agencies also attended. The International Atomic Energy Agency (IAEA) was present in attendance (UN YB, 1975).

The governments of the Netherlands Antilles, Papua New Guinea, and Surinam were represented at the conference by observers. The UN Commission on Human Rights (UNCHR) was also represented at the Conference by an observer. In accordance with GA Resolution 3276 (XXIX) of 10 December 1974, the representatives of the following national liberation movements attended the Conference as observers: the MPLA and FNLA; ANC; SWAPO; ANCZ; the MOLINCO; and the PLO (UN, 1976).

Eight intergovernmental organisations—the Commission of the European Communities (CEC), the Council for Mutual Economic Assistance (CMEA), the International American Commission on Women (IACW), the Inter-American Development Bank (IADB), the LAS, the OAU, and the Observatory of Economic Complexity [OEC] (Ibid).

In accordance with the ECOSOC decision 73 (LVIII), 114 non-governmental organisations also attended the Conference. The conference was convened by the Secretary-General of the UN and was opened by the President of Mexico, Luis Echeverria Alvarez. Following the opening address, the Conference elected Pedro Ojeda Paullada of Mexico as its President and Maria Groza of Romania as the Rapporteur-General (Ibid, 120-121).

Then, the Conference elected 46 Vice-Presidents comprising Asian and African countries, from the following countries: Argentina; Bulgaria; Canada; China; Colombia; Cuba; Dominican Republic; Ecuador; France; Gabon; German Democratic Republic (Germany); Greece; Grenada; India; Indonesia; Italy; Ivory Coast; Japan; Kenya; Mauritius; New Zealand; Niger; Nigeria; Norway; Pakistan; Panama; Peru; Philippines; Poland; South Vietnam; Somalia; Sri Lanka; Sudan; Sweden; Syrian Arab Republic (Syria); Thailand; Tunisia; Ukrainian

Soviet Socialist Republic; USSR; UK; U.S.; Venezuela; Yugoslavia; Zaire; and Zambia (International Women's Year, 1975).

After electing the officers, the Conference established two committees. These committees were formed to examine the Conference's substantive agenda. Committee I was chaired by Jean-Martin Cisse of Guinea, while Shapour Rassekh of Iran chaired Committee II (Ibid).

On 1 July 1975, Committee I of the Conference considered and approved without voting a draft World Plan of Action (also known as the Declaration of Mexico on Equality of Women and Their Contribution to Development and Peace) on implementing the International Women's Year. Composed of thirty principles, this plan crystallised the past and present long-term objectives of the movements under the Conference's theme—Equality—Development—Peace (Ibid).

The Conference urged governments to establish short-term, medium-term, and long-term targets to implement the plan. At the global and regional levels, it recommended that 'the UN proclaim the decade of 1975 to 1985 as the UN decade for women and development to ensure that national and global action be sustained' (UN, 1976).

The purpose of the Plan was mainly to stimulate national and international action to solve the problems of underdevelopment and of the socio-economic structure, which placed women in an inferior position, and to achieve the goals of International Women's Year (Hollins-Digital Commons). It was designed to translate into practical reality the principles of the Universal Declaration of Human Rights and the Declaration on the Elimination of Discrimination against Women (Symonides et al. 1999).

In addition, the Conference also adopted thirty-five (35) resolutions supplementing the World Plan of Action. These resolutions addressed various women's issues. For instance, by the resolution on the status of women in South Africa, Namibia, and Zimbabwe, the conference vigorously condemned the minority regimes of South Africa, Namibia, and Zimbabwe for their obstinate policy of oppression and contempt for the efforts of the UN and patience of the international community (International Women's Year, 1975).

The Conference, further, expressed its support for the oppressed inhabitants of South Africa, Namibia, and Zimbabwe in their national struggle for the total eradication of Apartheid; and also, invited the Secretary-General of the UN and all the UN specialised agencies to initiate studies on the influence of Apartheid on the status of women and to present a report to the GA's Special Committee on Apartheid and the Commission on the Status of Women (Ibid).

The Conference, furthermore, urged all states, UN organisations, and intergovernmental and non-governmental organisations to support the inhabitants of Southern Africa by adopting measures, including implementing UN resolutions bearing on the elimination of racism, Apartheid, racial discrimination, and the liberation of inhabitants under colonial domination and alien subjugation. It, therefore, appealed to all States to provide full support and assistance, morally and materially, for the victims of Apartheid and racial discrimination and the national liberation movements (Ibid).

## *5.3 Conclusion*

This chapter focussed on the effects of the representation of national liberation movements at the UN. One major finding of the chapter is that the admission of the movements into the UN system resulted in the world body acknowledging them as partners in global matters. As discussed, the UN acknowledged the role of liberation movements by inviting, alongside member States, representatives of the movements to participate regularly in the conferences organised under its auspices, alongside the member States. As illustrated, the liberation movements participated in the First Session UN Diplomatic Conference on the Reaffirmation and Development of IHL (1974); the UN Conference on the Representation of State Relations with International Organisations (1975); and the World Conference on International Women's Year (1975). As discussed, it was the OAU-recognised national liberation movements that participated in those conferences—the FNLA and MPLA; SWAPO; ZAPU, and ZANU; FRELIMO; ANC, and PAC.

# CHAPTER SIX

## Summary, Evaluation and Conclusion

### 6.1 Summary

Indeed, the UN is one of the international forums in which leaders of the revolutionary or national liberation movements have been represented. Utilising a wide range of sources—primary and secondary, this book has sought to analyse the representation of Southern African national liberation movements at the UN, from 1962 to 1975. The study focused primarily on the practise for the movements' representation at UN; UN reaction and respond to the movements' representation over time; role of the OAU on the representation of the movements at the UN; and the effects of the representation of the movements at the UN. In so doing, this study goes beyond current historiography on national liberation movements in several ways. To begin with, there have been no studies, which have approached the representation of national liberation movements at the UN through an analysis of their activities as a single entity on the international political plane, through to the independence and freedom of their countries and people.

The central purpose of this study has been to provide fresh insights into the role of national liberation movements in the UN. In part, it has done so by breaking from the tendency in the current literature to treat the disjointed, regional liberation movements' involvement with the UN. This has meant that important themes in African history have been overlooked. One key consequence of this tendency has been the ignoring or neglecting of the role of national liberation movements in the region as a single entity in the UN. By taking a 'long view' of the activities of these movements at that level, this study has provided a framework to link or weave together their previously disjointed history. Although the subject of national liberation movements has attracted a huge scholarly interest, the perspective provided in this thesis has shed new light on the germination of the seed for representation of the movements of the region in international institutions, particularly at the UN. Furthermore, by analysing activities of the national liberation movements at the international level provides a deeper understanding of their strategies for mobilising aid and support, their diplomatic struggles, the international community's perceptions of them, and their overall role in global politics

## 6.2 Evaluation

Chapter two dealt with practice for the representation of the national liberation movements at the UN. The chapter has revealed that there were no explicit provisions or pertinent rules of procedure for the representation of national liberation movements during the formative years of the UN. It has also been noted that the rules and procedures for representation of the liberation movements at the UN evolved out of the authorising decisions of the GA and ECOSOC. The chapter has illustrated, *Inter alia*, that the practice was that the representatives of liberation movements were invited through the OAU, and invitations were transmitted by the Secretary-General after the decision to invite them had been taken by the relevant GA organ or committee. It has also revealed that such practice arose primarily from the UN GA organs or committees—the Fourth Committee of the GA, the Special Committee on Independence, the UN Council for Namibia and the ECA. It has further showed that FRELIMO, ZAPU, and ZANU, MPLA, FNLA, SWAPO Namibia, ANC, and PAC were all represented in those committees and organs.

Chapter Three focussed on the UN reaction and response to the representation of the national liberation movements over time. The chapter has shown that the international community reacted and responded to the representation of the national liberation movements by acknowledging their role in the decolonisation process. It has also revealed that the role was expressed through the UN GA's decisions that offered international aid and support to the liberation movements. It has also been noted that the UN took those decisions in consultation and cooperation with the OAU. The chapter further illustrated that the necessary arrangements for the liberation movements to take part in the UN proceedings and deliberations were funded by the GA, through the Secretary-General. It has, moreover, showed that the UN General Assembly's decisions and voting (1965-1974) explicitly endorsed national liberation movements as key partners in decolonisation discussions.

Chapter Four of the study concerned the role of the OAU in the representation of national liberation movements at the UN. The chapter has revealed that it was because of threat to African peace and security, violation of inalienable rights, and opposition to the principles of self-determination and independence resulting from apartheid and colonialism, that the OAU decided to assist and support the national liberation movement in Africa—thereby contributing to the representation at the UN. It has also illustrated that the movements were those in Namibia, Zimbabwe, Angola, Mozambique, and South Africa, and revealed that the OAU supported the liberation movements diplomatically. The chapter has further that the OAU recognised the national liberation movements as authentic representatives of colonial countries. Moreover, it has noted the extent of OAU decisions on support and aid for the liberation movements. The chapter further that decisions by the OAU's Executive Council (Council of Ministers and the Assembly of Heads of State and Government) regarding assistance and support for liberation movements significantly contributed to their representation at the UN.

The Fifth Chapter concerned the effects of the representation of national liberation movements at the UN. It has been revealed that the liberation movements' admission resulted in their increased international recognition and involvement with the world body. The chapter has also noted that the increased international recognition of the national liberation movements was acknowledged when the UN invited OAU-recognised movements to participate on a regular basis in the conferences organised under its auspices. It, has further, noted that the FNLA and MPLA (Angola); SWAPO (Namibia); ZAPU, and ZANU (Zimbabwe); FRELIMO (Mozambique); ANC and PAC (South Africa) that were represented in the UN Diplomatic Conference on the Reaffirmation and Development of International Humanitarian Law Applicable in Armed Conflicts [IHL] (1974); the UN Conference on the Representation of State Relations with

International Organisations (1975); and the World Conference on International Women's Year (1975). The chapter has further revealed that the statements or proposals and amendments made or submitted by delegations of the national liberation movements were circulated by the conferences as their documents.

## 6.3 Conclusion

The representation of Southern African national liberation movements at the UN significantly impacted international affairs. Yet their representation in the world body is not reflected in the current literature. There has been a tendency in the historiography to focus on individual liberation movements' involvement with the UN, rather than discussions focussing on the movements as a single entity on the international political plane. Such an approach ignored the direct relevance of events or phenomena that preceded the independence and freedom of the people in colonial countries. Further, the collective legacy and experiences of the representatives of liberation movements' international life also had an influence on the formulation and implementation of the post-independence and post-freedom African foreign and domestic policies. This study goes beyond the current historiography by bringing a new perspective, arguing that there has been an oversight on activities of national liberation movements of the Southern Africa region as a single entity in international organisations, the UN in this regard. Specifically, the thesis answers the following questions: What was the practice for the representation of national liberation movements at the UN? How did the UN react and respond to the representation of national liberation movements over time? What was the OAU's role in the representation of national liberation movements at the UN? Most importantly, what were the effects for representation of national liberation movements at the UN? This conclusion aims to tentatively suggest an answer. Several theoretical cases may be made in favour of the effects of the representation of national liberation movements at the UN. For instance, it could be done through an examination of the international community's recognition of the national liberation movements. The OAU crafted the recognition of national liberation movements. It required a minimum level of effectiveness and representation of the movement concerned, before UN acceptance and, to exclude in practice 'secessionist movements' while ascertaining their representativeness (Mastorodimos, 2016). However, the OAU practices for recognition showed high levels of subjectivity within its criteria, notably the representativeness of the liberation movements and the degree of effectiveness regarding the existence of armed struggle. Some of the recognised movements were, in fact, not engaged in any armed struggle (Ibid).

Despite that, the OAU recognitions were 'readily' and 'incontestably' accepted by the UN GA. For instance, and as highlighted earlier, the assembly in its resolutions recognised the national liberation movements of Angola, Guinea-Bissau, Cape Verde, Mozambique, Zimbabwe, Namibia, and South Africa as the 'authentic representative of the peoples' of those territories. In fact, many states even recognised the national liberation movements and allowed them to establish official representation in their territory and provided them with moral and material assistance (Olalia, 2004).

UN recognition of liberation movements as "legitimate representatives" did not equate to governmental recognition. But it allowed them a certain level of protection under international law; enabled them to purchase weapons and other equipment; gave them access to financial resources; and strengthened possible reparation claims for damages they suffered during the civil war (Czapliński, 2016). According to Uchegbu (1977), the foundation and recognition of the liberation movements were themselves a creation of states exercising their sovereign rights—thereby making them assume international obligation, albeit in their mutual relations. Although it was declaratory regarding its purpose, recognition of the national liberation movements was also constitutive regarding its outcomes (Mastorodimos, 2016).

The UN admitted the liberation movements as 'quasi-governmental' organisations, while regional organisations such as the OAU admitted them as 'states' (Ibid) or *proto-states* (Suy, 2002). This implied that the representatives of the movements were permitted to represent those people at the international level, even though they were not in control of the territory (Jadarian, 2007). The quasi-recognition of the liberation movements enhanced their diplomatic status. This would be given substance by the UN Conference on the

Representation of States in their Relations with International Organisations (1975), and the final act of the Conference, which called upon the GA to examine the general question of observer status of the movements (Silverburg, 1977).

Some viewed UN recognition of national liberation movements as anathema to traditional legal thought, fearing it could lead to a revised international procedural code for global affairs (Lal Panjabi, 1989). Others observed that recognition within the UN and in State practice of the liberation movements altered the traditional distinction between internal conflict and international conflict in that it extended the scope of international humanitarian law (Prize, 1988).

Further, the national liberation movements' recognition reflected developments in the new international legal order of the last half of the twentieth century in which the right to self-determination had become entrenched in the *Jus cogens*, basic, fundamental, imperative, or overriding rules of international law, peremptory norms which could not be set aside by treaty or acquiescence but only by the formation of a subsequent norm of contrary effect (Berat, 1990).

Moreover, recognition by UN bodies of the national liberation movements meant that the struggle against colonialism and apartheid in Southern Africa was legitimate as far as the purposes and principles of the Charter and other declarations were concerned (El-Ayouty, 1972). The UN recognition of the national liberation movements resembled recognition of a government in line with its legitimacy or a government-in-exile, in the event of total lack of territorial control (Guzel, 2019). But it differed substantially from classic forms of recognition in international law (Mastorodimos, 2016).

Despite that, UN recognition of the liberation movements was significant for their legal standing. The recognised movements, therefore, could possess 'limited' legal personality and would possess certain rights and obligations under international law. Violations of these international duties and obligations would, consequently, incur legal consequences at the international level. It gave them a legal capacity to use force and apply international law in national liberation conflicts, in contrast to terrorist organisations (Trevona, 2007). The national liberation movements 'legal capacity to use force was unanimously accepted but was not met with universal agreement because it was only recognised by newly independent States and socialist countries, while countries faced with such conflicts did not so (Prize, 1988). Despite this, the use of force by liberation movements to gain self-determination and independence became legal in terms of international law (Higgins, 2004).

The GA granted the OAU recognised national liberation movements observer status in its proceedings and deliberations on colonial matters. It also allowed representatives of the liberation movements to participate regularly in the conferences organised under UN auspices. Accordingly, this move aligned with the demands of people striving for national liberation and the practical conduct of their activities within the UN and other organisations (UN, 1986). Granting the national liberation movements observer status and the associated opportunities, privileges, and immunities (e.g. enjoying the status of a head of state) also became a reasonable product of the practical need for the people struggling for their liberation to take part in the activities of the UN and other universal-membership international bodies (Ibid). Such status also signified the limited legal personality of the national liberation movements (Trevona, 2007). Also, by granting the liberation movements the status of observers, the Assembly recognised them as responsible representatives of the peoples in their respective territories and, through them recognising, the right which those people had to form an independent state (Faundez, 1989).

The observer status, privileges, and immunities, in turn, gave the national liberation movements much greater access to the UN. These were not purely symbolic because, over the years, liberation movements had made an important contribution to the formulation of UN policy, not only in matters directly concerning decolonisation, but also in more general social and economic matters (Ibid). The national liberation movements were thus also able to participate in the deliberations and proceedings of other UN organs, as well as the SC. For instance, under its rules of procedure, the ECOSOC had, since 1969, invited the OAU-recognised national liberation movements to participate, without the right to vote, in its deliberations on matters of particular concern to those movements UN, 1992).

In 1972, the SC extended an invitation to certain individuals who were also members of the national liberation movements to participate in its work. Those persons included, among others: Amilcar Cabral (PAIGC); Peter Mushihange (SWAPO); M. Luvalo and M. Santos

(FRELIMO); Potlako Leballo (PAC); Alfred Nzo (ANC, South Africa) and George Silundika [ZAPU] (UN Library). In 1973, the Human Rights Commission (HRC), an ECOSOC organ, recommended full-scale moral and material assistance to liberation movements, liberated territories, and their populations (E/RES 19—XXIV, 1973). Other specialised agencies and UN-related organisations, such as UNESCO; the Food and Agricultural Organisation (FAO); the World Health Organisation (WHO); and the International Labour Organisation (ILO), also adopted the GA's policies relating to the liberation movements (Shaw, 1983). In 1974, the GA invited as observers regularly representatives of national liberation movements recognised by the OAU to participate in the relevant work of its main committees and its subsidiary organs, as well as in meeting, seminars and conferences, held under the auspices of the UN whenever they related to their countries—including the necessary arrangements for their effective participation such as requisite financial provisions (UN YB, 1974). In 1975, the UNDP established a National Liberation Trust Fund, a development, which coincided with the independence of Angola and Mozambique from Portuguese colonial rule. This fund would be utilised by the remaining dependent territories in Southern Africa (Zimbabwe, Namibia and South Africa) until their independence. The National Liberation Trust Fund was administered in close collaboration with the OAU and the host governments of the countries where the national liberation movements were based. Part of the assistance to refugees from the colonial territories granted by the United Nations High Commissioner of Refugees (UNHCR) was also channelled through liberation movements recognised by the OAU (E/RES 1804—LV, 1975).

By emphasising the representation of Southern African national liberation movements at the UN, and by treating and or prioritising the movements as a single entity in their involvement with the entire system of the organisation, this book provides an analysis of the liberation movements' role on the international political plane. Representation of national liberation movements on the international political stage remains a contentious topic, intersecting politics, law, and international relations. This meeting point started to emerge in 1962 when the GA, through the Special Committee of 24, decided to implement the 1960 Declaration on Decolonisation. By 1975, a significant precedent was set regarding the representation of Southern African national liberation movements at the UN.

# References

"Observer Status of National Liberation Movements Recognised by the OAU and/or League of Arab States," Report of the Secretary-General, *Document: A/41/534*, Item 124 of the Provisional Agenda, Forty-First Session, United Nations General Assembly, 8 September 1986, p.6.

"Participation of National Liberation Movements: Rule 73", *Document 5715/Rev.2*, Rules of Procedure of the Economic and Social Council, United Nations, New York, 1992, p.28.

A/RE/2908—XXVII. 1972. Implementation of the Declaration on the Granting of Independence to Colonial Countries and People, adopted at the 2079th Plenary Meeting, 2 November 1972, https://undocs.org.

A/RES/2105—XX, 1965. Implementation of the declaration on the granting of independence to colonial countries and peoples, adopted at its $1405^{th}$ plenary meeting, on 20 December 1965. http://www.worldlii.org

A/RES/2189—XXI, 1966. Implementation of the declaration on the granting of independence to colonial countries and peoples, adopted at its $1492^{nd}$ plenary meeting, on 13 December 1966. https://documents-dds-ny.un.org

A/RES/2621—XXV, 1970. Programme of action for the full implementation of the declaration on the granting of independence to colonial countries and peoples, adopted at the $1862^{nd}$ plenary meeting, on 12 October 1970. http://www.worldlii.org

A/RES/2627—XXV, 1970. Declaration on the occasion of the twenty-fifth anniversary of the United Nations, adopted at the $1883^{rd}$ plenary meeting, on 24 October 1970. https://digitallibrary.un.org

A/RES/2674—XXV, 1970. Respect for human rights in armed conflicts, adopted at the $1922^{nd}$ plenary meeting, on 9 December 1970. http://www.worldlii.org

A/RES/2708—XXV, 1971. Implementation of the declaration on the granting of independence to colonial countries and peoples, adopted at the $2028^{th}$ plenary meeting, on 20 December 1971, adopted at the $1929^{th}$ plenary meeting, on 14 December 1970. https://documents-dds-ny.un.org

A/RES/2787—XXVI, 1971. Importance of the universal realisation of the right to self-determination and the speedy granting of independence to colonial countries and peoples for the effective guarantee and observance of human rights, adopted at the 2001$^{st}$ plenary meeting, on 6 December 1971. https://tamilnation.org.

A/RES/2795—XXI, 1971. Question of territories under Portuguese administration, adopted at the 2012th plenary meeting, on 10 December 1971. https://www.refworld.org

A/RES/2852—XXVI, 1971. Respect for human rights in armed conflicts, adopted at the 2027$^{th}$ plenary meeting, 20 December 1971. https://www.refworld.org

A/RES/2878—XXVI, 1971. Implementation of the declaration on the granting of independence to colonial countries and peoples, adopted at the 2028$^{th}$ plenary meeting, on 20 December 1971. http://www.worldlii.org

A/RES/2908—XXVII, 1972. Implementation of the declaration on the granting of independence to colonial countries and peoples, adopted at the 2078$^{th}$ plenary meeting, on 2 November 1972. https://digitallibrary.un.org

A/RES/2909—XXVII, 1972. Dissemination of information on decolonisation, adopted at the 2078$^{th}$ plenary meeting, on 2 November 1972. https://digitallibrary.un.org

A/RES/2918—XXVII, (1972). Question of territories under Portuguese administration, adopted at the 2084$^{th}$ plenary meeting, on 14 November 1972. http://www.worldlii.org

A/RES/2918—XXVII. 1972. Question of the Territories under PortugueseAdministration.Adoptedatthe2084thplenarymeeting, 14 December 1972, http://www.worldlii.org.

A/RES/2955—XXVII, 1972. Importance of the universal realisation of peoples to self-determination and the speedy granting of independence to colonial countries and peoples for the effective guarantees and observance of human rights, adopted on the 2107$^{th}$ plenary meeting, on 12 December 1972. http://www.worldlii.org

A/RES/3102— XXVIII, 1973. Respect for human rights in armed conflicts, 2197$^{th}$ plenary meeting, on 12 December 1973. https://israelipalestinian.procon.org

A/RES/3103— XXVIII, 1973. Basic principles of the legal status of the combatants struggling against colonial and alien domination and racist regimes, adopted at the 2197$^{th}$ plenary meeting, 12 December 1973. https://www.refworld.org

A/RES/3111—XXVIII, 1973. Question of Namibia, adopted at the 2198th plenary meeting, on 12 December 1973. http://www.worldlii.org

A/RES/3111—XXVIII. 1973. The Question of Namibia. Resolutions adopted on the recommendation of the Fourth Committee, 2198th Plenary Meeting, 12 December 1973, https://undocs.org.

A/RES/3115—XXVIII), 1973. Question of Southern Rhodesia, adopted at the 2198th plenary meeting, on 12 December 1973. http://www.worldlii.org.

A/RES/3115—XXVIII. 1973. The Question of Southern Rhodesia. Resolutions adopted on the recommendation of the Fourth Committee, 2198th Plenary Meeting, 12 December 1973, https://undocs.org.

A/RES/3151G—XXVIII. 1973. Situation in South Africa Resulting from the policies of Apartheid. Adopted at the 2201st Plenary Meeting,14December1973,https://digitallibrary.un.org.

A/RES/3163—XXVIII, 1973. Implementation of the Declaration on the Granting of Independence to Colonial Countries and Peoples, adopted at the 2202nd plenary meeting, on 14 December 1973, United Nations. https://digitallibrary.un.org

A/RES/3280—XXIX, 1974. Cooperation between the United Nations and Organisation of Africa Unity, adopted at the 2312th plenary meeting, on 10 December 1974. https://documents-dds-ny.un.org

Ade-Ibijola, A.O. et.al. 2020. The East-West Ideological Struggle and the Politics of African Decolonisation in the United Nations: Historical Analysis, *Issues in Social Sciences*, Volume 8, No.2, Macrothink Institute, p.59.

African National Congress (1973, August). Oslo Conference on Colonialism and Apartheid. *Sechaba, Official Organ of African National Congress South Africa*, Volume 7 &, No.8, pp.4-5.

AHG/Res.25 (II), 1965. Southern Rhodesia. OAU, Addis Ababa, Ethiopia.

AHG/Res.35 (II), 1965. Territories under Portuguese Domination. OAU Secretariat, Addis Ababa, Ethiopia.

AHG/Res.7 (I), 1964. Apartheid and Racial Discrimination. OAU Secretariat, Addis Ababa, Ethiopia.

AHG/Res.9 (I), 1964. Territories under Portuguese Administration.

Akiwumi, A.H. 1972. The Economic Commission of Africa,*Journal of African Law*, Volume, 16, No.3, London School of Oriental and African Studies, p.254.

Aldrich, R. and Cornell, J. 2006, *The Last Colonies*, Cambridge, p.158.

Alexander A. 2016. International Humanitarian Law, Postcolonialism and the 1977 Geneva Protocol I, *Melbourne Journal of International Law*, Volume 17, No.1, University of Melbourne.

Asian-African Consultative Organisation. https://aalco.int

Asmal, K. 1984. The legal status of national liberation movements with particular reference to South Africa, United Nations Digital Library, https://digitallibrary.un.org.

Ataman, M. 2003 (Fall). The Impact of Non-State Actors on WorldAnnual Report (1 March 1960-February 1969), Document E/4651, *EconomicandSocialCouncilRecords*, Forty- Seventh Session, United Nations, New York, 1969, p.145.

Barber,H.W.,(Fall)1975.DecolonisationCommitteeofTwenty-Four,*World Affairs*, Vol. 138, No. 2, Sage Publications.

Barker, R.R. (Winter) 1975. Humanitarian Law or Humanitarian Politics? The 1974 Diplomatic Conference on Humanitarian Law, *Harvard International Law Journal*, Volume 16, No.1.

Barker, R.R., 1975 (Winter) Humanitarian Law, or Humanitarian Politics? The 1974 Diplomatic Conference on Humanitarian Law, *Harvard International Law Journal*, Volume 16, No.1, p.14.

Bartelson, J. 2013 (March). Three concepts of recognition. *International Theory*, Volume 5, Issue 1, Cambridge University Press, p.127.

Berat, L. 1990 (November). Namibia: The Road to Independence and The Problem of Succession of States. *Journal of Political Science*, Volume 18, No.1, Article 10, p.40.

Binaisa, G.L. 1977 (July). Organisation of African Unity and Decolonisation: Present and Future Trends. *The Annals of the American Academy of Political and Social Science* (432), Africa in Transition. Sage Publications, Inc. in association with the American Academy of Political and Social Science, p.58.

Boavida, I. et.al. 2010. *The Emperor of Ethiopia in Lusoland: Haile Selassie's state visit to Portugal in 1959 and the Birth of the OAU*. Centro de Estudos Africanos, Portugal, p.41.

Britz, A.B. 2011 (December). The Struggle for Liberation and the Fight for Democracy: The Impact of Liberation Movement

Governance on Democratic Consolidation in Zimbabwe and South Africa. *MA Thesis*, Stellenbosch University, p.34.

Brolman, C. (2007). *The international veil in public international law: International organisations and the law of treaties*. Oxford: Hart Publishing.

C/Res.300 (XXI), 1973. Declaration on Territories under Portuguese Domination. OAU Secretariat, Addis Ababa.

Casalin, D. and Lamb, C. 2008. Participation of States in the International Conference of the Red Cross and Red Crescent and Assemblies of other International Organisations. *International Review of the Red Cross*, Volume 876, p.747.

Centre for Conflict Resolution. 2007. The United Nations and Africa: Peace Development and Human Security, *Policy Seminar Report*, University of Cape Town, South Africa, and the Friedrich Hebert Stiftung, Mozambique 14 - 16 December 2006, Hotel Avenida, Maputo, Mozambique.

Clapham, A. 2017. Human Rights Obligations for Non-State-Actors: Where are We Now? *Draft Article*, Volume 6, Issue 7, Graduate Institute of International and Development Studies, p.2.

CLAS/Plen.2/Reve.2, 1963. Agenda Item II—Decolonisation. OAU Secretariat, Addis Ababa, Ethiopia.

CM.Res.96 (VIII), 1967. Resolution on Southern Rhodesia. OAU Secretariat, Addis Ababa, Ethiopia.

CM/Res. 206 (XIII), 1969. Resolution on Decolonisation and Apartheid.

CM/Res. 207 (XIV), 1970. Resolution on Zimbabwe. OAU Secretariat, Addis Ababa, Ethiopia.

CM/Res. 209 (XIV), 1970. Resolution on decolonisation and Apartheid, OAU Secretariat, Addis Ababa, Ethiopia.

CM/Res. 271 (XIX), 1972. Resolution on the Report of the Co-ordinating Committee for the Liberation of Africa. OAU Secretariat, Addis Ababa, Ethiopia.

CM/Res.101 (IX), 1967. Resolution on the Territories under Portuguese Domination. OAU Secretariat, Addis Ababa, Ethiopia.

CM/Res.108 (IX), 1967. Resolution on Southern Rhodesia. OAU Secretariat, Addis Ababa, Ethiopia.

CM/Res.13 (II), 1964. Apartheid in South Africa. OAU Secretariat, Addis Ababa, Ethiopia.

CM/Res.135 (X), 1968. Resolution on Southern Rhodesia. OAU Secretariat, Addis Ababa, Ethiopia.
CM/Res.137 (X), 1968. Resolution on Territories under Portuguese Domination. Secretariat, Addis Ababa, Ethiopia, February 1968.
CM/Res.138 (X), 1968. Resolution on Southwest Africans Tried and Sentenced in South Africa. Addis Ababa, Ethiopia.
CM/Res.14 (II), 1964. Southern Rhodesia. OAU Secretariat, Addis Ababa, Ethiopia.
CM/Res.142 (X), 1968. Resolution on Southwest Africa. OAU Secretariat, Addis Ababa, Ethiopia.
CM/Res.150 (XI),1968. Resolution on Namibia. OAU Secretariat, Addis Ababa, Ethiopia.
CM/Res.153 (XI), 1968. Resolution on Rhodesia. OAU Secretariat, Addis Ababa, Ethiopia.
CM/Res.241/Rev.1 (XVII), 1971. Resolution on Decolonisation. OAU Secretariat, Addis Ababa.
CM/Res.242/Rev.1 (XVII), 1971. Resolution on Apartheid and Racial Discrimination. OAU Secretariat, Addis Ababa, Ethiopia.
CM/Res.267 (XIX), 1972. Resolution on Zimbabwe. OAU Secretariat, Addis Ababa, Ethiopia.
CM/Res.268 (XIX), 1972. Resolution on the Portuguese Colonies.OAU Secretariat, Addis Ababa, Ethiopia.
CM/Res.269 (XIX), 1972. Resolution on Namibia. OAU Secretariat, Addis Ababa, Ethiopia.
CM/Res.270 (XIX),1972. Resolution on Apartheid and Racial Discrimination. OAU Secretariat, Addis Ababa, Ethiopia.
CM/Res.298 (XXI), 1973. Resolution on Zimbabwe. OAU Secretariat, Addis Ababa, Ethiopia.
CM/Res.300 (XXI), 1973. Resolution on Namibia. OAU Secretariat, Addis Ababa, Ethiopia.
CM/Res.31 (III), 1964. Apartheid in South Africa. OAU Secretariat, Addis Ababa, Ethiopia.
CM/Res.33 (III), 1964. Southern Rhodesia. OAU Secretariat, Adds Ababa, Ethiopia.
CM/Res.34 (III), 1964. Territories under Portuguese Administration., OAU Secretariat, Addis Ababa, Ethiopia.
CM/Res.342 (XXIII), 1974. Resolution on South Africa and Namibia. OAU Secretariat, Addis Ababa, Ethiopia.

CM/Res.350 (XXIII), 1974. Resolution on Decolonization. OAU Secretariat, Addis Ababa.

CM/Res.62 (V), 1965, Southern Rhodesia. OAU Secretariat, Addis Ababa, Ethiopia.

CM/Res.62 (V), 1965. Southern Rhodesia. OAU Secretariat, Addis Ababa.

CM/Res.66 (V), 1965. Apartheid and Racial Discrimination in the Republic of South Africa. OAU Secretariat, Addis Ababa.

CM/Res.67 (V), 1965. Territories under Portuguese Domination. OAU Secretariat, Addis Ababa, Ethiopia.

CM/Res.77/Rev.1 (VII), 1966. Resolution on the OAU Co-ordinating Committee for the liberation of Africa. OAU Secretariat, Addis Ababa, Ethiopia.

CM/Res.78 (VII), 1966. Resolution on Southern Rhodesia. OAU Secretariat, Addis Ababa, Ethiopia.

CM/Res.86 (VIII), 1966. Resolution on Apartheid and Racial Discrimination. OAU Secretariat, Addis Ababa, Ethiopia.

CM/Res.87 (VII), 1966. Resolution on Southwest Africa. OAU Secretariat, Addis Ababa, Ethiopia.

CM/ST.13 (XXVII), 1974. Declaration. OAU Secretariat, Addis Ababa, Ethiopia.

Coguery-Vidrovitch, C. 1972 (December). *National liberation movements and decolonization in Africa south of the Sahara*, United Nations African Institute for Economic Development and Planning, Dakar, p.1.

Cristescu, A. (1981). *The right to self-determination: Historical and current developments on the basis of the United Nations instruments*, A study prepared by the Aureliu Cristescu, Special Rapporteur of the Sub-Commission on the Prevention of Discrimination and Protection of Minorities, United Nations, New York, p.9.

Czapliński, W. 2016. Recognition and International Legal Personality of Non-State Actors, *Pécs Journal of International and European Law*, No.1. p.9.

Decolonisation, 1975.*A Publication of the United Nations Department of Political Affairs: Trusteeship and Decolonisation*, Volume II, No.6, United Nations, New York, p.30.

Diplomatic Conference on the Reaffirmation and Development of International Humanitarian Law Applicable in Armed Conflict. (May) 1974. *International Review of the Red Cross*, Fourteenth Year.

Dunn, E. 1973 (Spring). OAU and the Mozambique Revolution. *A Journal of Opinion*, Volume 3. No.1, p.31.

Economic Commission for Africa. Annual Report (1 March 1968-14February1969) 1969.VolumeI,*EconomicandSocialCouncilOfficial Records*, Forty-Seventh Session, United Nations, New York, p.69.

EconomicCommissionforAfrica.AnnualReport(15February1970-13 February1971)1971.VolumeI,*EconomicandSocialCouncilOfficial Records*.

ECOSOC Resolution 974 D (IV)—Terms of reference of the Economic Commission for Africa: Membership", Resolutions adopted by the Council during its Thirty-Sixth Session, 1299$^{th}$ Plenary Meeting, 30 July 1963, https://undocs.org.

El-Ayouty, Y. (1972, Winter). Legitimization of national liberation: The United Nations and Southern Africa. *Journal of Opinion, 2*(4), 14 African Studies Association.

El-Ayouty, Y., & Hugh, C. (Eds.) (1974). *African and international organisation*. The Hague, Netherlands: Martinus Nijhoff.

El-Khawas, M.A. 1978. The Quite Role of OAU in Africa 's Liberation. *New Directions*, 5 (2), Article 7, p.16. https://dh.howard.edu/newdirections/vol5/iss2/7.

Emerson, R. 1965. Colonialism, Political Development, and the UN.

Faundez, J.1989.International Law and Wars of National Liberation: Use of Force and Intervention, HeinOnline, Available at: https://heinonline.org.

Forsythe, D.P. (January)1975. The 1974 Diplomatic Conference on Humanitarian Law: Some Observations, *American Journal of International Law*,Volume 69, Issue 1.

Fourth Committee of the United Nations. Collection Number AD1715. *Historical Papers Research Archive*, University of Witwatersrand, Johannesburg, South Africa.

Godsee, K. 2012. Rethinking State Socialist Mass Women's Organisations: The Committee of the Bulgarian Women's Movement and the United Nations Decade for Women, 1975-1985. *Journal of Women's History*, Volume 24, No.4.

Gorelick, E. 1986 (March). Apartheid and Colonialism. *The Comparative and International Law Journal of Southern Africa*, Institute of Foreign and Comparative Law, p.77. https://www.jstor.org/stable/23905613.

Gouraige, G.J.E. 1974 (April). The United Nations and Decolonisation,*The Black Scholar*, Volume 5, No.7, Taylor & Francis, pp.16-23.

Graham, E.D. 1975. The Diplomatic Conference on the Law of War: A Victory for Political Causes and A Return To the 'Just War' Concept of the Eleventh Century,"*Washington and Lee Law Review*, Volume 32, Issue 1, pp.31-32.

Guidelines for implementation of General Assembly Resolutions Granting Observer status on a Regular Basis to Certain Regional Intergovernmental Organisations, the Palestinian Liberation Organisation and the National Liberation Movements in Africa. 1975. *Extract from United Nations Judicial Yearbook*, Part Two. Legal activities of the United Nations and Related Intergovernmental Organisations, United Nations, New York, pp.164-167.

Guzel, M.S. 2019. "An Internationally Recognised National Liberation Movements-TMT", *ZFWT*, Volume 11, No.2, p.127.

Higgings, N. 2004. The Application of International Humanitarian Law to Wars of National Liberation, Journal of Humanitarian Assistance, http://www.jha.ac.

Higgins, N. 2004 "The Approach of International Law to Wars of National Liberation", *Monograph 3,* Martin Monograph Series, The Martin Institute, University of Idaho, p.30.

Higgins, N. 2004. Regulation of Armed Non-State Actors: Promoting the Application of the Laws to Conflicts involving National Liberation movements, *Journal of Humanitarian Assistance*, Feinstein International Centre, Tufts University, p.10.

Hollins Digital Commons, International Women's Day, https://digitalcommons.hollins.edu. *International Organisation*, Volume 19. No.5, p.493.

International Women's Year, 1975 (01 January-00:15:00) 1975. United Nations Audiovisual Library, United Multi-Media, https://unmultimedia.org.

Jadarian, D. 2007. International Humanitarian Law's Applicability to Armed No-State Actors. *A Graduate Paper*, University of Stockholm, p.23.

*Judicial Yearbook of the United Nations*, 1974. Office for Inter- Agency Affairs and Coordination, p.151.

Lal Panjabi, R.K. 1989 (Fall). International Law and the Use of Force by National Liberation Movements," Book Review, Denver *Journal of International Law and Policy*, Volume 18, No.1, Article 8, Fall 1989, p.143.

Lande, G. R. (1966). The effect of the United Nations General Assembly. *World Politics, 19*(1), 84.

Lazarus, C. (Anee] 1974. Le statut des mouvements de libérationnationale à l'Organisation des Nations Unies, 20, AnnuaireFrançais de Droit International.

Legum, C. 1975 (April). The Organisation of African Unity-Success or Failure. International Affairs, Volume 51, No.2, p.215.

Lovelace, A. 2014. When Global Governance Wins: The Role of the United Nations in Decolonization. *UC Merced Undergraduate Research Journal*, Volume 7, No.2, p.74

Mastorodimos, K. 2016. National Liberation Movements: Still a Valid Concept to International Law? *Oregon Review of International Law*, Vol.117. 71, pp.78-79. https://core.ac.uk/download/pdf/36693717.

McDougal, M.S. et. Al. 1975. Human Rights for Women and World Public Order :

The Outlawing of Sex-Based Discrimination. *Yale School of Legal Scholarship Repository*, Volume 1, Yale Law School.

Mittelman. J.H. 1976 (March). Collective Decolonization and the U.N. Committee of 24. *The Journal of Modern African Studies*, Volume 14, No.1, p.41.

Moses, A.D., Duranti, M. & Burke, R. 2020. *Decolonisation, Self- Determination and the Rise of Global Human Rights Politics*, Cambridge University Press, p.113.

O'Sullivan, C. (2005). The United Nations, decolonisation and self- determination in cold war sub-Saharan Africa, 1960-1994. *Journal of Third World Studies*, 22(2), University of Florida, 103.

Ogbu, E.O. 1983 (August). Towards A U.N. Strategy. Statement by His Excellency Ambassador E.O. Ogbu, Chairman: U.N. Special Committee on Apartheid at the Oslo Conference, *Sechaba*, Official Organ of the African National Congress, South Africa, 7 (8), London.

Olalia, E.U. 2006. The Fundamental Right of People to Struggle. *Dissent*,

Olcott, J. 2017. *International Women's Year: The Greatest Consciousness- Raising Event in History*, Oxford University Press.

Pap, D.S. 1978. Angola, National Liberation and the Soviet Union,*Parameters, Journal of the US Army War College*, p.26.

Paterson, M. 2013. African Union at Ten: Problems, Progress, and Prospects. Centre for Conflict Resolution, *Report*, p.6. https://www.jstor.com/stable/resp05177.5.

Pillay, P. 2000. The Geneva Conventions and the South African War of Liberation, *Alternation*, Volume 7, No.2, United Nations Centre, pp.148-154.

Politics: A Challenge to Nation-State. *Alternatives, Turkish Journal of International Relations*, Volume 2, No.1, p.46.

*Press Release*, 1974 (September). Public Library of US Diplomacy.

Prize, P.R. 1988. "International Law and the Use of Force by National Liberation movements," Books and Reviews, International committe e of the Red Cross (ICRC), https://international-review.icrc.org

*Records*, Fifty-First Session, Supplement No.5, United Nations, New York, p.2.

Report of the Fourth Committee. 1972. Document A/8933, Agenda Item 66, *Official Records of the General Assembly Annexes*, Twenty- Seventh Session, New York, p.3.

Report of the Fourth Committee. 1972. Document A/8957, Agenda Item 64, *Official Records of the General Assembly Annexes*, Twenty- Seventh Session, New York, p.2.

Report of the Special Committee on the Granting of Independence to Colonial Countries and Peoples. 1975. Volume III, Supplement No.23, Document A/9023/Add.3, *General Assembly Official Records*, Twenty-Eight Session, United Nations, New York, p.108.

Report of the United Nations Council for Namibia. 1972. Volume I, *General Assembly*

*Official Records*, Twenty-Seventh Session, Supplement No.24 (A/8724), New York, pp.29- 31.

Ruto, S.J., et.al, 2009. Promises & Realities: Taking Stock of the Third UN International Women's Conference", African Centre for Technology Studies, Nairobi, Kenya, African Women and Child Feature Service, http://www.awcfs.org.

Santos, A. A. E. (2012, January). The role of the Decolonisation Committee of the United Nations Organisations in the struggle against Portuguese colonialism in Africa: 1961- 1974. *The Journal of Pan Africanist Studies*, 4(10), Santa Clarita, California, p.252.

Santos, A.A.E, et.al. 2017. International Solidarities and Liberation of the Portuguese Colonies. *Afriche e Orienti*, Anno XIX, Numero 3, p.50. www.cormune.bologna.it/iperbole/africheorienti.

Schewed, A. 1982. Territorial Claims as a Limitation to the Right of Self-Determination in the Context of the Falkland Dispute. *Fordham International Law Journal*, Volume 6, No.443, p.452.

Shaw, M. 1983. The international status of national liberation movements. *Liverpool Law Rev* 5, https://doi.org.

Shimiyu, V. G. (1997). African nationalism and the struggle for freedom. In *Elija Masindi: A biography* (pp. 178-179). Nairobi, Kenya: East African Educational Publishers.

Silverburg, S.R. 1977. "The Palestine Liberation Organization in the United Nations: Implications for International Law and Relations", *Israel Law Review*, Volume 12, No.3, p.382.

Statue of the International Court of Justice, 1945. San Francisco, 1945, https://popp.undp.org.

Suy, E. 2002. New Players in International Relations, *Transnational Association*, Volume 3, p.166.

Symonides, J. et.al. 1999. *Human Rights of Women: A Collection of International and Regional Normative Instruments*, UNESCO, France.

Tekle, A. 1988 (3rd Quarter). Tale of Three Cities: The OAU and the Dialectics of Decolonisation. *Africa Today*, 35 (3/4), The OAU at 25: The Quest for Unity, Self-Determination and Human Rights, Indiana University Press, p.59.

Terretta, M. 2012. We were Fooled into Thinking that the UN Watches over the Entire World: Human Rights, UN Trust Territories, and Africa's Decolonisation. *Human Rights Quarterly*, Volume 34, No.2, 2012, p.1.

Tervona, H. (2007). "Self-Determination, National Liberation Movements and the Use of Force", *Durham E-Theses, Master of Jurisprudence*, Department of Law,

Durham University, p.31.

Tervona, H. 2007. "Self-Determination, National Liberation Movements and the Use of Force", *Durham E-Theses, Master of Jurisprudence*, Department of Law, Durham University, 2007, p.32.

*The Black Scholar*, Vol. 5, No. 7, African Liberation, p.18.

The Representation of National Liberation in the United Nations Organs: Legal Opinion prepared For the Under-Secretary-General Office for Inter-Agency Affairs and Coordination, 1974. *United Nations Judicial Yearbook*, New York, pp.149-153.

The Representation of National Liberation Movements in the United Nations: A Legal Opinion Prepared for the Under-Secretary-General, Office for Inter-Agency Affairs and Coordination, 1974. *Judicial Yearbook of the United Nations*, United Nations, New York, p,151.

Trevona, H. 2007. Self-determination, national liberation movements and the use of force, *Durham E- Thesis*, Master of Jurisprudence, Department of Law, Durham University, United Kingdom, p.29.

Uchegbu, A. 1977. Armed Struggle for National Liberation and International Law, *The African Review: A Journal of African Politics, Development and International Affairs*, Volume 7, No.1, University of Dar es Salaam, p.65.

Uchegbu, A. 1977. Armed Struggle for National Liberation and International Law, *The African Review: A Journal of African Politics, Development and International Affairs*, Volume 7, Issue 1, Dar E-salaam, Tanzania, pp.60-85)

Ukodang, O. (1971). The role of the new states in international law. *Archiv des Völkerrechts*, 15. Bd., No. 2, Mohr Siebeck GmbH & Co. KG, p.182.

UN (June-July) 1975. World Conference of the International Women's Year, Mexico City, Document E/CONF.66/5, Item 11 of the Provisional Agenda, HollinsDigital Commons, https://digitalcommons.hollins.edu.UN (June-July) 1976. Resolutions and Decisions adopted by the Conference: The Status of Women in South Africa, Namibia, and Southern Rhodesia. Document E/CONF.66/34, *Report of the International Women's Year, Mexico City*, New York.

UN Conference on the Representation of States in Their Relations with International Organizations. (March) 1975. Document: A/CONF.67/SR.1, Vienna, Austria.

UN Conference on the Representation of States in Their Relations with International Organizations, 1974-75. World Legal Institute, http://www.worldlii.org.

UN Conference on the Representation of States in Their Relations with International Organizations (March) 1975.Document: A/CONF.67/SR.5, *Extract*. Volume I, Official Records,UN Conference on the Representation of States in Their Relations with International Organizations, Vienna, Austria.

UN GA RES/3072 [XXVIII]. (November) 1973. United Nations Conference on the Representation of States in Their Relations with International Organisations. United Nations Documents, www.undocs.org.

UN GA Resolution 2966 [XXVII] (December) 1972. International Conference of plenipotentiaries on Representations of States relations with International Organisations. Document: A/8796, *Agenda Item 87,* Twenty- Seventh Session. New York.

UN, (June-July) 1976. Attendance and Organisation of Work. *Report of the World Conference of the International Women's Year,* Mexico City, New York.

UN, 1976. Resolutions, Applications of the Convention in Future Activities of International Organisations. Document: A/10141, *Request for the Inclusion of an Item in the Provisional Agenda,* Thirtieth Session, New York.

UN,1976. Official Records, Volume II. Document: A/CONF.67/10 and add.1, UN Conference on the Representations of States in their Relations with International Organisations, Vienna.

UN. (March) 1975.Documents: A/CONF.67/12, A/CONF.67/13/ and add.1 and A/CONF.67/14 United Nations Conference on the Representation of States relations with International Organisations, ILC, Twenty-Third Session, Vienna, Austria.

UN. (September) 1974. Document: A/9669. Report of the Secretary-General,

UN. 1976. Document: A/CONF.67/18, *Official Records,* Volume I. New York.

United Nations (1967). *Yearbook of the United Nations.* New York, pp. 5-6.

United Nations Trusteeship Council, 1950. Examination of Petitions, Fifth Report of the Ad Hoc Committee on Petitions, T/L.75, https://digitallibrary.un.org.

United Nations, 1961. *Yearbook of the United Nations,* New York, p.46.

United Nations, 1962. *Yearbook of the United Nations,* New York, p.58.

United Nations, 1968. *Yearbook of the United Nations.* New York, p.664.

United Nations, 1969. *Yearbook of the United Nations. New* York, pp. 635- 638.

United Nations, 1971. *Yearbook of the United Nations,* 1971. New York, p.58-519.

United Nations, 1972. *Yearbook of the United Nations.* New York, pp. 544- 548.

United Nations, 1973 *Yearbook of the United Nations.* New York, p.865.

United Nations, 1974, *Yearbook of the United Nations,* New York, p.663.

United Nations, 1974. *Yearbook of the United Nations.* New York, p.866.

United Nations, 1974.The representation of national liberation movements in United Nations organs: Economic Commission for Africa, *Extract,* United Nations Judicial Yearbook, Office of Legal Affairs, p.154.

United Nations, 1975.*Yearbook of the United Nations,* New York, p.164.

United Nations, 1976. *Yearbook of the United Nations.* New York, p.130

United Nations,1947. *Yearbook of the United Nations,* ` New York. p.223.
United Nations,1952. *Yearbook of the United Nations,* New York, p.52.
United Nations,1970. *Yearbook of the United Nations.* New York, pp. *707- 712.*
Valladares, G. The 1975 Mexico World Conference on Women, Origins: Current Events in Historical Perspective, Origins, The Ohio State University, https://origins.osu.edu.
Verhoeven, S. (March) 2007. International and Non-International Armed Conflicts. *Working Paper,* No 107, Institute for International Law, KatholiekeUniversiteit Leuven Faculty of Law.
Waldeman, S. 1975. Armed Struggle in Zimbabwe: A Brief Chronology of Guerilla Warfare, 1966-1975. *Ufahamu: A Journal of African Studies,* Volume 5, No.3, p.4.
Wibowo, M.R. 2021. The Relationship Between International Relations and International Law in The Aspects of International Politics. Faculty of Law, Universitas Muhammadiya, Indonesia, https://researchgate.net/publication/351 127540.
*World Affairs,* Volume 138, No.2, p.128.
Worster, W.T. 2007. Law, Politics, and the Conception of the State in State Recognition Theory, *Boston University International Law Journal,* Volume 27, No.1, p.124.
Yousuf, H.S. 1985 (Fourth Quarter). The OAU and the African National Liberation Movement. *Pakistan Horizon,* Vol. 38, No. 4, Pakistan Institute of International Affairs.

# Index

## A

Afghanistan, 51, 54, 55, 61, 62, 63, 64, 65, 66, 67, 68, 72
African Group at the UN, 15, 93, 97
African National Congress, xiii, 18, 139, 146
Angola, xiii, 15, 16, 18, 19, 21, 23, 25, 26, 30, 32, 35, 36, 37, 38, 39, 45, 46, 47, 58, 60, 65, 68, 91, 95, 96, 97, 98, 99, 103, 129, 131, 134, 146
Arafat, Yasser, 16, 17

## B

Banana, Canaan, 33
Barre, Mohamad Jaalle Siyad, 43

## C

Cabral, Amilcar, 16, 27, 40, 47
Cape Verde, xiii, 16, 27, 37, 38, 39, 46, 64, 65, 131
Commonwealth Ministers' Conference, 94
Comoros National Liberation Movement, 110
Conference of the International Women's Year, 71, 148, 149
Czechoslovakia, 64, 65, 66, 68, 72, 119

## D

Dada, Ould, 109, 111
Dar es Salaam, 32, 36, 45, 148
Declaration on the Granting of Independence to Colonial Countries and Peoples, 18, 29, 92, 139

Diplomatic Conference on the Reaffirmation and Development of International Humanitarian Law Applicable in Armed Conflicts, 70, 129
Djibouti Liberation Movement, 110

## E

Economic Commission for Africa, xiii, 43, 144, 149

## F

Food and Agricultural Organisation, xiii, 43, 134
Fourth Committee, xi, 23, 24, 26, 27, 28, 29, 30, 31, 32, 33, 34, 39, 48, 52, 58, 61, 65, 66, 67, 68, 72, 106, 128, 139, 144, 146
FRELIMO, xiii, 18, 27, 28, 30, 32, 33, 36, 38, 39, 40, 45, 48, 60, 62, 94, 96, 103, 110, 125, 128, 129, 134

## G

Geneva Conventions of 1949, 70, 74, 75
Goor, Canon Raymond, 27
Guinea-Bissau, 16, 38, 45, 46, 47, 60, 65, 72, 94, 98, 99, 103, 112, 131
Gurirab, Theo-Ben, 28, 41
Guyana, 29, 40, 62, 63, 64, 66, 67, 71

## H

Hambro, E, 113
Hove, Richard, 29

## I

Inter-American Development Bank, **123**
International American Commission on Women, **xiii, 123**
International Bank for Reconstruction and Development, **58, 91**
International Defence and Aid Fund, **30**

## K

Kambode, Jackson, **41**
Kinshasa, Democratic Republic of the Congo, **45**

## L

League of Arab States, **70, 117, 137**
Liberation Committee of the O.A.U, **79, 83, 86, 87, 88, 90, 99**
Luvualu, Pascal, **36**

## M

Madagascar, **34, 44, 62, 63, 64, 65, 66, 67, 68, 72, 118**
Mallik, T., **113**
Mandela, Nelson, **85**
Mbaeva, Veiue N, **31**
Morocco,, **28, 59, 61, 62, 66, 67, 68, 118**
Movement for the Liberation of Sao Tome, and Principe, **32**
Movement for the National Liberation of Comoro, **117**
Mozambique, **xiii, 15, 16, 18, 19, 21, 23, 25, 26, 27, 28, 33, 35, 36, 37, 38, 39, 45, 46, 47, 58, 60, 65, 68, 94, 95, 96, 97, 98, 99, 103, 129, 131, 134, 141, 144**
Mudzi, Mukudzei, **31**
Mushihange, Peter, **28, 29, 33, 133**

## N

National Front for the Liberation of Angola, **18**
Neto, Agostinho, **36, 45**
Ngwenya, Jane, **29**
Nkomo, Joshua, **83, 85, 86, 87**
Non-Self-Governing Territories, **57**
North Atlantic Treaty Organisation, **xiii, 60**
Nujoma, Sam, **41, 42, 43, 45, 46, 60**

## O

OAU Conference of Ministers, **45**
Organisation of African Unity, **xi, xiii, 15, 140, 145**

## P

Palestinian Liberation Organisation, **xiv, 16, 109, 145**
Popular Movement for the Liberation of Angola, **32**
Portuguese Administered Territories, **83, 84, 89, 91, 92, 98**
Provisional Revolutionary Government of the Republic of South Vietnam, **112**

## R

Revolutionary Council of Somalia, **43**

## S

Santos, Marcelino dos, **25, 27, 28, 39, 45, 56, 60, 62, 81, 133, 147**
Schaefer, Gordon, **27**
Self-determination, **16, 17, 18, 27, 28, 32, 38, 49, 51, 52, 53, 54, 58, 59, 60, 61, 65, 66, 73, 75, 79, 80, 82, 84, 87, 89, 90, 93,**

98, 100, 102, 108, 113, 129, 132, 133, 137, 138, 143
Seychelles People's United Party, 110
Sisulu, Walter, 85
Sithole, Ndabiningne, 83, 85, 86, 87
Smith, Ian, 89, 91, 94
Somali Coast Liberation Front, 110
South Africa, xiii, xiv, 16, 18, 19, 21, 30, 32, 36, 37, 38, 40, 43, 44, 45, 47, 52, 55, 58, 66, 68, 73, 81, 82, 83, 84, 85, 88, 89, 90, 95, 96, 97, 100, 101, 102, 106, 110, 111, 124, 129, 131, 134, 139, 140, 141, 142, 143, 144, 146, 148
South West Africa, xiv, 18, 26, 31, 40, 46, 89, 92
South West African National Union, xiv, 33
Southern Rhodesia, 33, 35, 37, 55, 58, 68, 73, 81, 84, 85, 87, 139, 141, 142, 143, 148
SWAPO, xiv, 18, 28, 29, 31, 33, 34, 36, 37, 38, 39, 40, 41, 42, 43, 45, 46, 48, 60, 62, 67, 92, 100, 101, 110, 117, 123, 125, 128, 129, 133

## T

Tambo, Oliver, 69
Thant, U., 54
The Hague Conventions of 1899 and 1907, 70, 75

## U

UN Conference on the Representation of State Relations with International Organisations, 105, 125, 130
UN Economic Commission for Africa, 23, 24, 43
UN General Assembly, 16, 20, 26, 48, 121, 129
UN High Commissioner for Refugee, 37
UN Security Council, 87, 92
UN Trust Fund for South Africa, 88, 90

Unilateral Declaration of Independence, 86
United Arab Republic, 40, 51, 55, 59
United Nations Development Programme, xiv, 58, 73
United Nations Education, Scientific and Cultural Organisation, 43
United Nations High Commission for Refugees, 43
Universal Declaration of Human Rights,, 59, 76
Universal Declaration on Human Rights, 53

## V

Victims of Colonialism and Apartheid in Southern Africa, 64, 69

## W

Waldheim, Kurt, 50
Working Group for the Development of Humanitarian Law, 110
World Conference on International Women's Year, 105, 122, 125, 130
World Health Organisation, xiv, 43, 134
World Peace Council, 27

## X

Xuma, A.B., 105

## Y

Yugoslavia, 34, 40, 51, 55, 56, 59, 61, 62, 64, 65, 66, 67, 68, 71, 72, 113, 115, 118, 124

## Z

Zimbabwe, xiii, 15, 16, 18, 19, 21, 23, 25, 26, 29, 30, 31, 32, 33, 35, 37, 38, 39, 47, 58, 60, 67, 73, 79, 82, 83, 84, 85, 86, 87, 88, 89, 90, 91, 92, 93, 94, 95, 96, 97, 98, 100, 102, 124, 129, 131, 134, 141, 142, 150

Zimbabwe African National Council, 33

Zimbabwean African People's Union, 18

www.ingramcontent.com/pod-product-compliance
Lightning Source LLC
Chambersburg PA
CBHW021759230426
43669CB00006B/134